© 2016 Edward Zapski   ALL RIGHTS RESERVED

Welcome!

This is a story of a love that has no beginning and no end, forever between the Author and reader.

From the first, a powerful enemy lied to you to have you break your relationship with the Author.

In this, the reader inherits a war that was not of your choosing, but will be won by the Author, and in that victory you may share.

You can choose love and life with the Author or enlist in the kingdom of the enemy.

In reading this book, you will know the Author, the enemy and yourself!

Edward – the writer

Table of Contents

Preface	ii
Define Your Terms	2
Reality	6
The Universe	10
Communication — Words	20
Institutions — gods of Evil	38
War	49
Origins — What and Who You Are	70
Christianity	97
Jeshua — the Christ	102
The Institution	111
Epilogue	125

Many years ago, the writer suggested the title "use your head for something besides a hat rack." The Author was not amused, but it is still good advice.

In another book (John 15-13) the Author exclaimed "Greater love has no man than this, that a man lay down his life for his friends." He spoke of himself, but doesn't it describe the American Marine?

The Writer - Edward

Preface

Before the fiction of time, there was war in the universe. The great *Angel of Light* drew a host of spirit beings to defy the Author and his hosts; the war endures.

Many millennia ago, in your human past, your biological mother and father chose the lie of the Angel and betrayed the Author. By that choice, they and you are born into that war against the Author.

All of the strife that humans call *wars* are battles in the unceasing cosmic war; you are either a willing pawn or a soldier.

Choose!

Define Your Terms

When you understand all of the principles that are presented here, you will truly have eaten of the tree of good and evil, or as you read on, you may learn how to partake of the Tree of Life!

1. All communication is metaphor, whether instinct or intelligence.

2. By words you will live or die, be deceived, or know truth.

3. Always define your terms; have words used with their precise, defined meaning. The Twister is your mortal enemy; on his terms he wins.

4. The abstract noun is a damnation of the English language; it can mean anything. Contrast with the Christ's Greek.

5. The deceived is always partnered in the deception.

6. Human justice is always had - right, more rarely done. Justice is a product of law; right is a product of God's spirit.

7. Everything is an absolute. How things relate

to each other is secondary to their existence. All reality is created absolute by an uncreated absolute.

8. Ignorance is universal and remedial; coupled with arrogance, it is fatal.

9. In all intelligent life, human and spirit, the right of choice is that which makes you in the image of God, whether a component or the essence of the soul.

10. Choice is the only unalienable right granted by God, but it presumes freedom which presumes liberty; that is where you attack the individual.

11. Things can be and not be at the same time within the same reality.

12. Parameters always change, not objectives.

13. It takes five votes to change the Constitution of the United States.

14. Those that demand loyalty are least likely to show any.

15. Prejudice is a universal survival instinct; only in the human is it wedded to choice and morality.

16. Society exists to deliver food and religion; both to be understood in a broad generic context.

17. All religions are an explanation of reality, and

in these positive and negative views, everyone chooses. Evolution is a religion.

18.   All institutions are intrinsically evil; subject to the Angel and his hosts.

19.   There is no natural law, only instincts, which in the human are subject to internalized law by conscience governed by choice.

20.   History is a chronicle of battles with peace, an illusory temporal state, while the Enemy prepares his pawns for the next battle.

21.   Anything is possible; God is not possible. God is a self-defined absolute

22.   There is alien life on the Earth. It is the few human beings chosen by the Author and bound to Him by choice. If you live in the Christ, you are not of this world.

23.   Science is not a search for truth; it is a search for understanding. Truth is a person, the Author Himself!

24.   Law implies promulgation and an originator.

25.   God has no partners; His software does not run on your computer.

26.   Prejudice is basic to all theories. Assumptions are made as fact and occasionally are subject to proof.

27. All humans are created unequal with an unalienable right to choose and be subject to the *consequences of choice*. Please note that the Author also exercises the right of choice.

28. There are none innocent. All are subject to the consequences of choice.

29. If you want to survive, be useful; if you want to prosper, be indispensable.

30. When you are born, prepare to die; when you are born, prepare to live forever.

Reality

Reality is an entity, the Continuum, whose boundaries from a beginning or non-beginning to an end or eternity are totally within the Author, who gives it existence.

The Author both encompasses and permeates all that is, and is in the Continuum. If He lifts His support of existence from the least of what is in the Continuum, it never existed, and every thing immediately is changed; all absolutes would have altered relationships. As it happens, in the economy of the Author, nothing is intrinsically lost. It is changed in form, components freed, power and energy lost or gained etc., not truly extinguished.

Three principles (however inadequate a word) are embedded in the operation of the Continuum. The first is motion. From a nano-particle, to a star system, to space, all are in motion and must be, for to stop, all would be darkness and death. A myriad of spinning universes are in every human and solid appearing rock (if you make a distinction between the two).

We define motion by a measure that we call time,

much as we may define space by a measure called inch. Time does not exist as an entity; stop all motion in the universe and there is nothing to measure.

If you accept that time does not exist in the Continuum, except as a descriptive term, then your perception of reality expands to take in existence of more dimensions, with their own rates of movement, and an interplay of all of these dimensions.

The thoughtful writers of the movie *Matrix* were right on target when they had personified beings moving from a parallel dimension to human and back again. This concept of parallel dimensions, and the fiction of time, will be useful in embracing the third principle.

The second principle of the Continuum, numbers, appears to the reader to be superficial; it is not! Your first thought might be that exponential multiplying each other to infinity proves that no material reality can exist by chance. Consider, rather, the absolute necessity for the perfection of numbers, to have things be as they are, especially in the unique existence of life on a planet: Earth!

The rate and changes in rate of expansion of the universe was an absolute in having stars, formed in number and character, to release the elements which ultimately form the material component of men and women. By the number, every galaxy must be in motion exactly as it is internally and externally; each of our planets moving exactly where they are and at their rates; the moon, also by the numbers, exactly as it is. It is by this cosmic calculus that the Continuum is made to be and so also, people. Numbers are the basis of discourse about all the science of the universe.

The third principle or pillar of the Continuum is the Eucharist, a word describing a person and an event in motion. So much of the Continuum is dedicated to making the elements of a material body, to be grafted onto a conscious spiritual entity, which causes him to know that he is alive and desires to know how and why. All other material life is alive, but doesn't know it.

What person is a prime construction of the Continuum and what event could pervade the existence? In that parallel dimension of motion, the Author chose, being that person who shared Divinity, to relinquish all the power of Reality so as to touch humanity as a kinsman in the flesh. Beauty, truth, perfection, was murdered, resurrected and

He returned with His blood to His Father. By that event, humans practicing choice could choose an alternate dimension, death and resurrection with Him.

By this person and this event, a species for whom much of the Continuum was made, could, by mutual choice, be wedded to its Creator. In all this power and magnificence of the Continuum, is it not awesome, that man can choose to reject as did Satan the Angel?

The Universe

In a genetically established 50,000 years, an apparently biological species, The Adamites, came into existence with a unique capacity to ask *what* and *why*. He did not question life, but rather his existence with a cosmic *why?*

We also have glimmers of the astonishing knowledge and scientific skills that he possessed in prehistoric millennia. The earth and its orbit around the sun, the planets, known in number and orbit, the exact calculation and usage of True North, the polestar, and much more that challenges science today.

All this knowledge needed to have been originated in intelligent beings much older than the Adamites, possessed of a spirit nature that permitted their movement from other dimensions of existence. Lacking a written text, it was easy to transfer an oral rendition of the Author's exact historic plan for the people, painted on the canvas of the heavens where symbols could be drawn to illustrate the total epoch of mankind, and the war in the heavens. Thus the star clusters, properly understood, are a complete pictorial representation of the oral history of mankind and the Author.

It is obvious that man would question and investigate his visible environment viz. all of the physical bodies of our solar system. However, evidence leaks in from prehistory, strongly suggesting lost science and knowledge communicated by other intelligent beings from elsewhere in the universe; the elsewhere may be no further than an alternate dimension.

How, then, do you proceed to understand yourself and your position in the universe? First, by not accepting the canon of religious science, which commands a doctrine based on theories presented as fact. Anything that suggests that the theory is in error is ignored or condemned, never debated or reported. Worse, opposition is attacked, exiled, and ruined; murder is not impossible as Galileo will testify. Once entrenched in a lie, the battle becomes truly vicious as becomes the children of the Angel; a liar and murderer from the beginning.

What we call the universe begins in nothing; a complex of unmeasured heat, light and energy, starting a fantastic journey, either mindless or incredibly purposeful, to the creation of biological life. This is a statistically impossible miracle! And yet, the reader may tremble at the notion that he and she are the rationale for all of this.

Science teaches that the early rate of expansion of the universe had to be exactly as it was for the stars formed to burn at exactly their temperature (neither too hot nor too cool) to form all of the elements that we know to be necessary to all biological life. When the stars collided and released their cascade of elements eventually to this minor planet in a minor galaxy, it was all there for us to become in a cosmic nanosecond.

So much more had to be numbers precise for this planet to be perfect for the human to be, and to thrive. The number of stars cannot be more or less, our galaxy must be the one, and planets must be in their exact mass, location, and orbit. The moon needs to exist and exist exactly where it is; all the numbers in the Continuum are and must be.

We are always learning more of how the Originator manages this exquisite, impossible perfection, focused on something even more awesome to comprehend; it is done for us! It is yours to choose to share in infinity

Perfection is one of the names of the Author acting in absolute infinit power. This action is viewed by humans as matter and energy, magnificently controlled by laws and principles, which bring order to all of the universe and the same in all its parts.

Not necessarily! Gravity may not exist at all in the periphery of the universe contained in the Continuum. Energy, if not created or destroyed, must have existed alone at the beginning, but energy did not create the universe and how do you know that energy is not annihilated in some part or periphery of the universe? The assumption made is an often repeated error viz. everything we observe and dignify as laws are exactly the same always and everywhere.

The universe is in a state of total and continuous chaos and every component is randomly chaotic (reference motion). All these chaotic elements exist individually and in random medians that relate in exponential numbers to each other to create an ordered, purposeful chaos in constant motion. This is an impossible statistical reality except that our rendering of chaos and the universe has its reality contained by its Originator in the Continuum.

Big Bang is a poor expression for a theory of how

the universe started on its evolutionary purposeful path, after it came into being. It makes no effort to explain the nothing from which it did not originate. Was it a word that created all that is, never less or more, but changing and recombining? Not only is a self-creating and recreating material reality statistically impossible, but your existence is the ultimate statistical absurdity. Kant would agree that, as long as one human being exists, he stands as a being both in and beyond the universe.

Consider that there are billions of cells comprising a human body and each cell universe has millions of chaotic elements in motion, unlike at any moment, than another cell that appears to have the same function. Further, these elements are resolved in billions of random medians which are associated with major medians, which we identify as having function, an intellectual concept unique in human persons that know that they are alive.

What has been described in the microcosm universe of the cell, directed to a predictable function, is statistically impossible. Expanded to all material reality, the identity of any function is non-definable by a 10 to endless power. A scientific conclusion could be that the cell does not exist, material life does not exist, the universe does not exist, and all material reality does not exist. Indeed, except for the constant power presence of the Author, no thing would exist; He is the Sustainer.

Consider a reader that chooses to absolutely deny the existence of Divinity, and his structural Continuum. Either she is the creator of herself first and then created the universe, or the universe created itself and then created the reader. But we determined that the universe cannot exist much less order random chaos into controlled function. Yet we have humanity with a degree of control by individual choice. Choice and the Creator is the end and the beginning viz. Person of God.

Somewhere in the pantheon of speculative scientific gods of the universe, you will find god Evolution. It offers a theory of why there are more species than one on Earth and why the wide variation in a species. In this theory, death is the deciding agent in the selection of what death determines to be fit for survival by choosing to keep chaacteristics that it likes in the genome. In this is an interesting explanation of variation in a species, but not so good for species transition wherein millions of genetic macro jumps over endless time would produce a new species. The time problem was resolved by the theory of genetic macro jumps by which thousands or millions of new life forms appear in a hypothetical few generations, i.e., a group of apes running about gave a sudden birth to a man and a woman.

The attraction of this theory, presented by Wallace and Darwin was that it got rid of the supranatural, God and religion *interfering* in scientific thought and weds the human to a dog, monkey or pig as an instinctive *intelligent* animal. However, Darwin attached a condition to validate his ideas viz. that billions of fossils of the sequence of transitional leaps would be found for each species. There were none that were a proven sequence: none!

One of the earliest proponents of evolution in the formation of some human sub-species was, of course, Muhammad. Under the direct supervision of supernatural beings, he identified Jews as genetic descendants of pigs and monkeys. Thus evolution is easily adapted to racial purity and gross impurity.

The recent memory of the Third Reich codified the cultural European convictions of racial superiority by scientifically (evolution) identifying the *pigs and monkeys* about us and to systematically remove the pollutants from contaminating the purity of the Nordic superhuman; the true blend of spirit and body. So much for theory turned into a religion to be promoted with vehemence unto death: Your death! Remember that if only the fit are appointed to live, then the unfit are appointed to die

A battle won by the human and spirit forces of the Angel of Light would certainly be celebrated by a total rejection of the Author, except in the gestalt of the Continuum, all promises are kept. A chronically suicidal Jewish nation saw the reality of a state born in the blood of millions as an impossible promise kept. How soon will you forget the cost and trade away the promise?

Now if the Author will indulge the writer, I will suggest another theory for the origin of life on earth and the subsequent origin of species. Evolutionists postulate that bacteria are the earliest material (is there any other?) life form living billions of years ago in sometimes toxic oceans. Recently a remarkable discovery was made indicating that bacteria communicate with each other to calculate the exact number necessary to overcome a given immune system and will not act until the logistics warrant the move; a truly amazing degree of planning, knowledge of their numbers, and deep knowledge about their target. We already know that they have arranged their genes and developed strains that can thrive in incredibly hostile and poisonous environments, where no other life can be. Why, then, can we not conclude that this is the super intelligent life that created all of the rest? These, then, are gods that employ strategy and tactics with military precision.

Deep in an asteroid was a frozen liquid bearing intelligent life forms plunging into our early ocean, flourising and adapting through myriad mutations, an exchange of what we call genetic material. Needing water to survive, they sought to widen the bounds of their existence by creating other water-based organisms as hosts; that would permit the bacteria to live on land with enhanced mobility. Initially, the hosts' functions were controlled by simple organic computers, much later to be more sophisticated in a variety of apes and a humanoid called Neanderthal. Still, none of these were up to the great plan the bacteria had envisioned from the beginning viz. colonizing the universe. For this they needed something special.

About 50,000 years ago, they made two bags of bacteria and water, a male and female, with a truly advanced computer in their heads. Additionally, they placed a virus called mitochondria in each host cell to maintain total control. While the equally intelligent pig and whale may have been early experiments, it became clear that these two apes called humans were especially suited to make the transports that would allow the bacteria that had completely colonized the earth, to spread out to all the systems in space.

The writer now decrees that this is the new and final religion of evolution. If you question, disagree, or attempt any contrary hypothesis, you will be ridiculed as a God idiot at best and destroyed at worst. This is the way of religious scions in our day and their tawdry universe peopled by bags of bacteria and water.

Think! There is a universe in the brain of each human; all different and all unique.

Communication — Words

In the beginning was The Word and The Word was with The God and The Word was God.

From the beginning, it is clear that there is a special cosmic significance to words that convey life from the Author or death by the Angel's skillful manipulation of the same words to destroy the Author's most precious creation: Mankind!

Reality depends on communication and indeed exhibits attributes of its nature through communication. In this action, all entities reveal much of what they must be; all individual and, by definition, unequal and therefore only subject to probability of action within constantly changing parameters. In response to changing circumstances, subatomic entities manifest particle, wave, energy, and many other characteristics that humans cannot comprehend. They can neither be absolutely located and measured because the fundamental principle of the universe is motion.

Time is a word that humans use to fix a linear measure of motion, and to measure a rate of motion when there is only continuous non-directional, multi-dimensional motion. Time, then, is an abstract conceptual noun that literally defines nothing, but is a useful invention first applied to the many cycles in the universe of which the moon calendar is an example.

It is proper to apply, as a principle of the universe, continuous communication, utilization of the energy of space for the transmission of information, and actionable relations with all other entities. The product of this interaction is the alteration of each of the colliding entities and possible production of different entities that continue the process of interaction. All of this action has all the aspects of random chaos, except, that it is also subject to the *laws* of probability.

It is not surprising that the human is completely captive to the necessity of communication, being another unique individual actor in the universe of interaction. A lightly regarded activity of the human is thought communication, an activity shared with The God. For the human, it seems necessary to be aware of forming ideas using words pictured mentally, but not sounded. Beyond this, a very unique emotion, love (a name of the God), can be transmitted instantly through unmeasured expanse to the receptive Being.

Consider that humans interact with the same apparently random chaos as do sub-atomic entities. Millions of contacts are made through all the senses and beyond, each individual and unequal, constantly changing the sender and the receiver; producing a shower of reactive communication bits that affect and change a myriad of other humans in an ongoing series of unpredictable consequences.

Now grasp this thought: each contact radiates and causes change throughout the universe in perpetual motion. The effects are variable and of unpredictable magnitude, never ending, and yet interacting continuously with billions of contacts. Thus, if a human animal could think and reason and *know* anything, it might conclude that it is an irrelevant communicator in a cosmos of motion. But this creature does abstract reasoning and knows itself both relevant and infinitely responsible for each of its communications, regardless of intent or lack of intent. In a previous book by the Author, this was made clear by the requirement of a *sin offering* for guilt which accrues to an individual's actions with unknown negative effects, which, however, are subject to the knowledge and evaluation of the Author.

Only with responsibility does good and evil have any moral meaning, always falling on the individual and uniquely in the human nature, by the absolute *right* of choice. Millions of choices are made by individuals that guide and modify instinct, manifest an awareness of moral self, and something called spirit, which can only be known by a creature with the capacity to reason in the abstract.

All communication results in a stream of change, whether good or evil, in any degree. For the individual, good and evil are the consequences of choices and the accompanying responsibility subject to the individual's morality in his choices.

Applying good and evil to individual choices is meaningless, unless you have implanted in you the knowledge of the Author and his standards for every personalized being. For the human the standards are simple and absolute: *Love God with your whole being and your neighbor as yourself.* Deny the parameters of Divinity and your choices are made only to satisfy your instincts.

Existence is seemingly a state of being which indeed is not a static state since it is subject to continuous motion and continuous change. It is had by all reality with different properties. Choice defines the human while indviduality is in common with all else. This unique *right* is limited to intelligent beings as it emanates from its shared possessor, the Author.

Since everything in the universe is individual, choice is an absolute right only as applied to the absolute of personified individualism

Freedom and liberty are rights of societal origin and absolutely necessary for the operation of choice, reacting to continuously changing parameters, but subject for good or bad, to definit on and limitation, by society's institutions. Society can deny you freedom and inhibit your choice, but even God will not recall the right. It is the only absolute right.

Rather than rights, it would be better to view freedom and liberty as absolutely necessary conditions for the exercise of choice in good judgment and total individual responsibility. Laws, rules, and regulations are all limits on freedom and liberty and thus restrict and penalize choice. Understand that elements in society, operating through institutions, exist to control the individual's choice to *insure* against *bad* choices for the *good* of society.

How the institution inhibits freedom and liberty depends on how it views the individual; usually as an evolved animal with an unexplained and frequently unused ability for abstract reasoning. Of course, instinct is another basic component of human identity, which in extreme circumstances, can operate independent of choice. However, the self-aware individual will modify and even negate instinct in favor of responsible choice. God views his creation, a supernatural being, in whom he has placed conscience to guide responsible choice. The Angel of Light and his enslaved servants in institutions of power are ruthless in placing these humanoid animals into herds under total control, except that they must overcome that burdensome right of choice.

Choice and right are words which bring life to a person, so an act of pure brilliance would be to have them bring death, and The Angel has always done just that. He wears a well-earned crown with the words "liar and murderer from the beginning." Words were the weapons that he used to wage war on God and his creation and certainly his nuanced use of God's right to life to inflict death on billions, not by his hand, but their own *choice*. This is the greatest height of achievement. As before, the woman was open to his explanation of her rights and choice, and it followed only to his national institutions to codify in law, the absolute right to kill inherent only in the woman.

Now the woman is like God, in that she determines who lives or dies, and she is to be worshipped as the giver of life: The woman is god!

This most successful salesperson of death, the Angel of Light, with his dominion over the earth, seeks to homogenize humanity, exercise control over all your choices, but only with your full consent (free will). Indeed humans are now evolved gods; some gods, with a superior intellect, destined to lead and define good and evil for all the others. The trick is to invite a change of mind from the *delusions* of a Divinity, later compelling the change by whatever force is necessary. His agents are adept by guiding you sensually to serve his version of universal social good, while joining his disciples in destroying all opposition to the great plan.

All of your life you will walk in a minefield of deception, clever lies and impossible promises; sensual *happiness* for the individual at the expense of society or *happiness* for society at the expense of the individual, with all surrendering their freedom of choice. It has always been comfortable to join, conform, compromise, and seek the anonymous security of the herd driven to serve his version of universal social good.

Be assured that God, in his spiritual creation, instilled the capacity to know right judgment compatible with the only two laws addressed to the individual, spirit-directed, reasoning human: *Love God with your whole being and your neighbor as yourself!* Here is introduced one of God's names that brings the reasoned meaning of love to a transcendent plane, not an ethical instinct. On this basis, the individual is to responsibly exercise choice and discrimination within the daily shifting parameters of his environment. Note that discrimination is nothing more than choice in constant daily practice.

Now you know what rights must flow from the Divinity of choice; free will and the individual are sacred, life and liberty must exist as rights to permit the free exercise of choice. If you live in a land devoted to freedom of the individual, then there is no true victim, except that he or she accepts that role.

Like choice, God created one more intrinsic capacity that functions in humans as a very special form of communication: Love, a supernatural capacity imbedded in our being, like radioactivity, that is released as showers of communication. They impart and change an infinite number of receivers and change the sender who is also a continuous receiver. It is not properly an emotion, but a very real capacity for special superhuman communication. It exists in all of God's supernatural beings and most importantly, an attribute and name of God from the beginning.

The writer was quietly thinking, "If I could reach out and just touch the Author very lightly," but indeed I could do more, radiate love throughout the universe of God's presence in a perfect exchange of communication; a wonderful exchange of love.

How then does the Angel break the communication and degrade this supernatural capacity? Easily: Render love an instinctive (animal) emotion, entirely limited to acts which perpetuate the species. Nurturing of the young, concern for the poor, the sick, etc., are only to be managed by chosen leaders, for the betterment of the whole with no individual's responsibility.

Choice information requires a supernatural, God-inspired, capacity in the individual to know and judge good and evil in a myriad of varying circumstances; to defy instinct when necessary to do the right. Good and evil are not objective entities, but abstract manifestations of subjective individual choice referenced to the perfection of God.

Buddhists do not acknowledge a transcendent God, and not surprisingly do not regard good and evil as reality, and indeed leave the question of realty to speculation. Also, they have no concept of individual as presented herein. Although appealing to Western sophisticates, this religion is too amorphous for significant use by haters of the individual. The religion of evolution is better at defining one animal product, human, responding only to instincts, neither good or bad, with a mythical illusion of choice.

The agents of the Angel exalt free will as the action principle of choice of *good* that satisfies, gives pleasure, assuages guilt, and accepts all that society defines as good. Superior beings need to control society with instincts deemed *useful* ordained, and those not useful evil. Thus, it is common to find good is evil and evil good as benefits the controlling institution that defines good and evil for its subjects.

With any of the wisdom that you may have gained from the Author, grasp the enormity of Divinity in this immense spiritual power of choice that opens beyond the material universe, and dwell on the person who made choices before the worlds were formed. Jeshua chose to submit *freely* to torture and death to pay a familial blood debt and also endured the full knowledge of that execution in every blood-soaked detail, until the cosmic moment when it was done. Did you understand *free will*: the purity of choice, the efficacy of the sacrifice by one individual – one person – Jeshua? The Angel knew full-well how choice could be twisted even in trying to induce the Christ to profane its use in exchange for all power in the world relinquished by Lucifer, only in exchange for worshipping the Angel. It began with an individual, totally responsible for the consequences of choice, ending with individuals and the consequences of their choices.

For the animal, all reality is interpreted by its species' genetic instinct, a totally automatic, non-thought process. As a human, I cannot comprehend reality without the absolute of Truth; understanding is not an instinct. For the evolutionary humanoid, there can be no truth or objective reality, for both have no meaning unless related to the Divinity. Bear in mind that Truth is the name of a person and his reality is only comprehended by the spiritual component of the created man. Only a spiritual intellect can discriminate in the abstract, to interpret and evaluate reality. The lie misrepresents truth to appeal to instinct, and recomposes reality to fit

Now let me introduce you to the curse of the abstract noun, words that are meaningless, except for their ability to ignite a rage of emotion, when employed by the most brilliant, Angel of Light. Under his guidance, you have found it easy to justify the destruction of the lives of people and nations.

Words are audio-metaphors, sounds which by teaching and traditional usage, permit a form of communication to convey abstract ideas by their specific meaning. They result in choice and action based on developed belief. You have already understood the Angel's brilliant corruption of the right of choice: Now view more of his vocabulary of lies. These words are ambiguous in themselves and rely on individuals for subjective emotional impact. They are meant to appeal to *higher instincts* (animal emotions?) in evolved humanoids. If some miserable humans relate to the God, Lucifer cleverly creates a meaning for his words, with seemingly Divine origin.

Nothing is equal anywhere is the Continuum. Persons have a defining right of choice, but it cannot function equally in a reality and universe of individuals and motion. Therefore, equality in the universe is an oxymoron (stress on moron). Inequality is a fundamental of existence.

Consider the Trinity, three individual persons, not equal, but individuals sharing the Godhead. Knowing this truth perfectly well, why would a superior being, the Angel of Light, cause all humanity to pursue that which doesn't exist?

By this word, he elicits hate and anger in individuals, to use revolution to homogenize humanity; no individuals, all equal, no choices, only the harmony of complete control of every aspect of life, including your *deserving* it.

There is no right to equality; it doesn't exist. No person is equal to any other in any respect. Every nano-second, the reader is not the person that he or she was. Every sub-particle in your body is in motion and changing. Thus, the pursuit of a non-existent equality to achieve dominance over all individuals, is effectively serving the will of the Angel.

When related to The God, equality can only suggest maximizing opportunity for the individual to be totally responsible for his choices and their consequences, known and unknown. Now you can see that freedom and liberty are not rights, but conditions for the exercise of the true right of choice by human and spirit persons.

Another murderous word is fair; impossible to define, but experienced emotionally and differently by each individual. It is an assumed right, like equality, which doesn't exist, and like equality, it is used to arouse envy, revenge, hatred, and *justify* the murder of millions, especially in our contemporary, enlightened times. Fair requires a victim and oppressor. The oppressor may be nature, destroying people in a catastrophe or a myriad of diseases.

Note, however, that there is no covenant for life and health in the natural world; everyone dies on terms not necessarily of their choosing. It is the spirit essence of a human that does not die. The victim cries out against discrimination and proclaims his deserved rights. Saul of Tarsus made clear that all deserve death, but can live through the blood merit of the one that truly deserves, Jeshua, the Christ. How *unfair* for an evolved animal that is miraculously conscious of its life, which is to end quickly in nothing!

Understand *right* as the exercise of God's perfection, and *justice* in its many forms is human law, that specifically avoids individual morality, and locks the masses in a vise of judgment, for the good of all, as determined by the institution. It is a coldly blind executioner of judgment that dispenses with consideration of individuals; professing to be non-discriminatory, it executes judgment to satisfy itself. Thus justice is always done, but right is rare. While the institution determines *right* for all, which defies definition, the individual doing God's right, validates justice. Paul made it clear that we are justified by Jeshua's *righteousness*, not institutional law.

When you make your reference point Divinity, not

an animal humanoid, all of these instinct-arousing emotional words will be replaced in the inspired man, with a conscience driven cry, *God's right be done*!

Two of the favorite words in the arena of Christianity and biblical discourse that the Angel embraces and manipulates through his institutional minions are faith (Faith) and church (Church).

There is no such thing as not operating on faith, which clearly makes this an action word; a verb. It is to be understood as acting on belief with confidence in that belief viz. *faithing*. If you wish to speak of belief, trust, or a religious institution, then do so, and not ambiguously, with the abstract noun – faith. Christian tradition speaks of *Faith, Hope and Charity* as biblical principles which, when viewed correctly, stand as the definition of faithing; acting on belief, with the certainty of truth, in total love. This is what the Christian individual does!

What, then, is the game that the Angel plays? He obscures the precision of Paul's use of the word and leads the institution to take faith with its many implied meanings and attach it to doctrine and tradition as biblical validation. Contemporary use implies meanings such as belief, trust, profession of membership, etc., all with the ambiguous noun in the assumed context. Did you ever ask why not teach the specifically correct words, instead of hiding in ambiguity?

What do you make of the word church? It's origin in the writing of the Author and Paul, translated from the Greek, identifies a people outcalled by God, as individuals offering themselves totally to God for His use, and in that, are made holy. Current floating use of the word searches the context for learned assumptions. A myriad of defintions now accrue to this word: an institution, corporate officers (hierarchy), a collective of members that *belong* to an institution, a building, which in tradition is a temple, and for some a meeting house for religious rites or discussions. Note the clever and effective usage of the word to tie to the Biblical text and completely obscure the original – intended – no accident! Tell me then, who is it that profits from this word game?

The Angel is not done, saying, "I shall bring down the names of God to the animals that you are." Indeed, he has done it!

Consider that Beauty is not "in the eye of the beholder," but in line, color, form, sound, emotion, all virtues that appeal to and are understood by a special creator possessing the spirit of Beauty – God! Lacking that spark, supreme ugliness is held up as the height of beauty. It is obvious that the animal cannot abstract the significance of such a word, much less its expression.

Love, which could properly be a pillar of the Continuum, is reduced to sexual adventures. Creator is replaced by a life-giving mother goddess. The pleasure and profit of evil is offered as right and good. The Devil's dictionary is truly ponderous.

He is a liar and murderer from the beginning, fashioning words to be instruments of death for the creatures that he hates and despises from the beginning.

Institutions — gods of Evil

Perhaps 50,000 years ago, there arose on the earth a person, the first of what genetically we are – humans! Uniquely intrinsic in this nature was individuality, self-awareness, and the remarkable ability to reason, question, and communicate ideas with an insatiable need to know all existence. As with the factor of intelligence, all survival instincts were managed absolutes: viz. food, security and reproduction.

With the passage of years, great civilizations rose and fell, victims of enormous catastrophes, leaving mathematical and astronomical records in store. An oral repository of all collective knowledge from human beginnings and their relations with non-human persons was often incorporated in what we call myths.

It is a critical telling point that this continuing thread of knowledge was preserved by priests and shamans as an inherited secret collection, including non-human sources. Again, from the first, there was a connection with supernatural beings that was dominant in the lives of each individual, as is quite evident even from a review of the recent history of 12,000 years. All of history is the story of the individual and how he has met or failed the fundamentals of his nature: instinct under control of a brain had for abstract thought and communication.

The first humans initiated a structure which we call societal civilization, and created institutions to make it workable. All of human needs were to be addressed by social units with the family as the initial basic institution. The extended family became the clan, tribe, federation, and nation, with a requisite increase in specialization and bureaucracy to regulate, control and domesticate the individual, *for the good of all*!

The two universal institutions, religious and secular, are unique human inventions, ideally indispensable structures for harmonizing relationships between individuals, in what is called society, and which ideally is a structure to permit the individual to utilize choice for maximum personal benefit. However, I would make the case that the institution, by its nature, is eternally hostile to the individual, for it requires the surrender of the only inalienable human right – choice!

I am god: you are to serve me and no other. I grow

in power through dominance and control. Worship me and I will keep you, if useful. When you fail me, I will destroy you for you are only an appendage!

This is the credo of the institution written by the great spirit power; ruler of the world. His quote, "Arbeit mach Frei," is a compliment to his way with words. By giving you the minimum of food and security, in a homogenized, anonymous mass of humanity, you survived. The only individuals in this human herd are ruthless elite of lesser gods that are the organic ruling members of the corporation. Some of the corporate elite choose to welcome powerful spirit beings to cohabit as advisors and protectors. Any individual who rejects submission, or even questions the authority of the elite, is branded an outlaw, a contamination to be destroyed.

There is almost a serenity in belonging to the dominant mob; a welcome relief from responsibility and choice, one ideology, no longer alone, but buried in the anonymity of the herd. Might you agree that most Muslims, Jews and Christians find more comfort in being embedded in a society rather than being *alone* with God?

The Angel's pick for leadership becomes convinced

that she and he are not only superior beings, but the only divinity that evolution has ever produced. They become a benevolent evil (oxymoron) doing evil when necessary, for the good of all others! It is always better that one should die rather than the corporation perish!

There are all kinds of prisons: criminal confinement, crippling illness, stupid regulation, dead end labor, etc., but the Angel wants to imprison your mind, your thought, your belief, your truth — your choice: that is how you lose your soul. For the herd, it offers the promise of social justice and total satisfaction for any conceivable wrong. The corporation that owns you will remake your mind and body to become gods; for the institutions that you serve are gods.

Religious institutions that allegedly speak with the voice of God, require total submissive membership for *salvation*. All choice and questions are strictly channeled into orthodox doctrine. Everyone outside of these bounds is a heretic to be silenced, most often by killing them. (Worthy of note: kings and rulers often claim absolute rights by Divine authority.) While the major religions vary from simple to detailed, complex in their basic tenets and associated rituals, the powerful corporations evolve and develop *infallible* accretions of tradition, which binds the individual to this society, and transfers identity and responsibility to the group. This is both inevitable and quite normal.

In our human animal form, we have receptors on our cells, locks if you will, of a certain shape to be filled by floating communication keys that facilitate *right* cell activity. But this human is a strange animal indeed, for it knows that it is alive and endlessly questions *why existence?* That is why there are *spiritual* receptors within our being, sometimes defined wrongly or rightly as conscience. These receptors are open to communication with Divinity to facilitate the knowing and doing of *right* by the individual. Secular institutions are adept at plugging the spiritual receptors with virtual and real drugs until God is effectively blocked. Perversely, the universal questions remain and the human lives in continuous unresolved stress. This is where the religious corporation steps in to promise real truth, final peace, and conditional salvation

How, then, are these purveyors of corporate truth different? They are not! These states, secular and religious, have always been entwined, and yet, necessarily at war with each other for dominance, although mutual accommodation is a common feature. These entities are virtual organisms that gain life through power and control, no less than humans need food.

What of the *good* person in these corporations? The best definition is to find the one doing the least harm. Doing what you should do has no special merit; the action completes itself, closing the circle. Obviously, there is no absolute standard to support the abstract idea of good, but doing *right* requires God and His standard; consequences, then, are what they are. Muhammad was correct when he observed that nothing he did (his works) guaranteed salvation.

Religions own people: you are not a member of a church, or Islam, or any; but you belong, are owned, by that entity. Thus, to leave or convert to another group is an intolerable act of theft, and all involved are punished severely as circumstances permit, unto death for heresy. So taught Aquinas, Dominic, the great Jewish sages and all imams starting with The Prophet Muhammad. Truth is continually defined and updated, and corporate officers tell you what must be believed in the rule of tradition, by Ulama, Church, Talmud, and Supreme Court of the United States.

An examination of history strongly suggests that Islam is the most consistently complete institution to take hold of mankind. The Quran subjects all government and every aspect of human life to its defined control and law. It is an absolute constitution, coexistent with Allah. Any challenge of its substance is an offense against Allah and punishable by death.

In absolute truth, this is a system of belief and action, brought to a chosen Arab by a powerful angel, either assumed or saying that he was Gabriel. Both before and after this encounter, spirit beings guided and protected Islam for fighting men to spread the commands of Allah to the world, by the word, whip, and sword, which they did with murderous enthusiasm and great profit

Eastern religions are strongly ethical and fatalistic in the pursuit of *good* lives, blending individuality (ego) with an abstract spiritual essence and often oblivion. They do not involve The God or an ambition to conquer the world which does not preclude them from occasional murderous battles. The individual is largely to accept the parameters of his life and submit gracefully. You might be surprised at what material profit does to this ideal

Western religious corporations are totally different in that they relate strictly to Divinity-God, although that person is defined with significant d ferences.

Christianity is amazingly simple and profound. Christ did not establish a corporation, but sent out teachers of Truth; Himself. The impossible Trinity; God sharing as a person, the Godhead with the person of the Father; the person of Jeshua; the person of The Holy Spirit. The Resurrection validates the Divinity of Jesus, and the promise of salvation by blood in his death. Most important is the insistent repetition of love in all the books of old and new, as the basic theme of God's relation to us. Certainly, it is love that validates our choice and action as right.

Islam and Hebraic religions view a more wrathful God, punishing repeated predictable failures with deadly catastrophes as well as individual disasters. For Hebrews, there was a remission of the transgressions by the shed blood of sacrificial animals in a ritual performed by a priest for the congregation. Islam absolutely denies the need of any blood sacrifices, and importantly, denies the blood sacrifice of Jeshua on the tree

Love, as it exists in the Continuum, is absent in the world of the Quran and its prophet, Muhammad. What is an insistent repeated command is the order to kill all disbelievers who fail to accept Islam. This enemy of Allah is the Christian, Jew, apostate, muslim, pagan, and any that do not accept the Quran, Hadith, and Muhammad, who brought the eternal book from the Angel to a disorganized tribal world.

In the process of Islam dominating the then world, the African and Eastern Orthodox Church were reduced to a sometime tolerated Christian remnant, except for Constantinople. Now it was the Roman Church corporation which became supreme, cleverly playing Western rulers to grow its power and theirs, as each jostled for advantage. The idea of unity was very effective.

The Angel of Light teaches that no nation is great without a strong, unified religious base. When the gods of Rome lost their luster, Constantine brought the unity and energy of Christianity into the Empire; so also did God permit the energy of Islam to create Ismael's great nation.

As much as Islam may be credited with the reduction of the Orthodox Christianity, it was Constantine who first established the institution, subject to his oversight, as the only state religion. Constantinople became the ruling center of Christianity, with Rome and Alexandria vigorously competing for power, but often allied against their common enemy.

In 732, a military stumble by Muslim forces in France initiated the leadership of a combination of Celtic tribes, finally raising up Charlemagne; like Constantine, committed to establishing the unity of one religion for his rule, which he pursued ruthlessly with great success. In 800, he was crowned Emperor of the Holy Roman Empire by the Pope in Rome; the Church, now the power in Europe, partnered with government, but always under the shadow of the Angel: CEO and Chairman!

In 1054, after centuries of political maneuvers, Rome's Pope saw Constantinople's isolation and decline, under constant pressure from Islam, while his strength in a dominant Europe was great enough for him to excommunicate the Orthodox Church. In this state, the Orthodox Church in Constantinople fell victim to attack by Venice with a wink from Pope Innocent III. This brilliant Pope controlled and subordinated all the kingdoms of Europe, the kings being vassals of Rome. The final insult came in 1453 with Islamic conquest and massacre of all in Constantinople, their heads decorating the celebrant's feast. All was watched with interest, but with no help from Rome.

Now we can understand institutions which seek a unity of a dehumanized world in which individuals are broken and remodeled for their own and societal good. In this process, note the terror and horror that all is done by law serving gods and man. Consider:

> The horror of the Inquisition — done by law!
> The murder of disbelievers — done by law!
> The horror of The Holocaust — done by law!
> The horror of abortion — done by law!

Contemporary technology makes all naked, stripped of individuality, and moved by mini-steps to a programmed stereotype by unstoppable blind algorithms. However, some of us are voluntary wards of a different entity; a person, upon whose word existence is, and whose word can consume his enemy, the corporation and their lofty leaders. It always remains for you to choose!

War

Within the context of the continuous cosmic war into which humans are born are the natural wars of all living biological creatures. Consider that from the moment of conception we are launched into a continuous biological war to the death, which we share with all organic creatures. On that level, the battle for food flows from your primal instinct to survive and reproduce. Killing to gain an advantage is routine, although pragmatic accommodations, often temporal, are also common. Although in human terms, food is not thought of as the accumulation of money, possessions, land, houses, etc., it certainly should be, for all can be turned into a food equivalent: The more, the better!

Death is a prominent component of wars, whether the death is of your cells and organs under the onslaught of viruses and bacteria, or a bullet lodged in your brain. But much of these biological battles can be applied to intelligent beings who uniquely devise weapons to temporarily halt the progression to inevitable death. Organic life on earth is limited to instinctive survival through protection and conquest of space and food supplies. These creature absolutes are clearly embraced in the history of humans based on the same needs.

It is well understood that the unpredictable shifts in the parameters of nature is the basis of murderous effects upon all life, which the theory of Evolution utilizes to highlight the ability of survivors to blindly use their unique characteristics to thrive in a new stabilized world; at least until the next onslaught. Since humans share life with all other creatures, the war with nature is one in which they have lost with catastrophic consequences during their short stay on earth.

Perhaps 20,000 years ago, the complete submergence of a continent situated over the Atlantic rift caused the extinction of a civilization, some of whose knowledge and science still eludes us in our time. That some escaped that destruction is clear from the myriad of myths held by natives of the Americas and unequaled mathematics and craft exhibited in stone.

Seventy-five hundred years ago, the civilizations of the Mediterranean and Black Sea were decimated by unimaginable flooding as a result of the collapse of dams at

Gibraltar (Jibral Tariq) and the Bosphorus which caused an enormous wall of water to drastically reshape the land and more drastically, the history of humans. Obviously, the event had worldwide consequences which are memorialized in a universe of myths. In all these events, there are intelligent beings understanding the danger pending from the enemy before it strikes and surviving with knowledge and science for new generations.

As the cosmic war is totally about power, control and human enslavement, so also are the human wars of choice; first to achieve the institutional control from which to distribute the stolen wealth to subjects and satisfy hate and revenge with an ideology usually absent The God. By the rules of this game, winners elevate their gods and destroy the gods of the enslaved.

The Author, by right of creation and possession, gifted Ibrahim and a chosen line of descendants with lands and promises that included the necessity of wars for Hebrews to take their assigned property from indigenous peoples. The Angel found the idea useful in making all the Muslim conquests the property of Al-Lah in perpetuity and when *stolen*, especially by Christian pagans, they must be restored by the reborn Islam. All the umma of Islam are holding their breath awaiting the one who will lead the conquest of the earth for Allah.

In a very real sense, these wars are revolutions; violent deadly actions to produce change, always chaotic and moving to a new unpredictable equilibrium. Many of these military adventures which were tribal encounters in the past are so at present; best understood as Mafia-like contests for territory and profit, albeit several million people may be killed.

Wars in which superior agents of the Angel are the guiding forces are those totally devoted to power and control with world domination the objective, bearing in mind that the defined world was different for Alexander, the Persians, Rome, and of course, Muhammad's Arabs flying the black flags of Islam

In this kind of war, the masses are bound by a supernatural fire, a violent religious zeal wherein one stands for the whole and the whole for one. The elite leaders and commanders of the faithful (believers) are considered God ordained. But if the ideology is Godless, then the elite are gods and goddesses requiring worship, adoration, and blood sacrifice; the individual disappears into a mass of committed slaves.

Reviewing this bleak picture of human choices, one stumbles on a remarkable aberration, a concoction of individualism, religious principle, and understanding of the Angel's influence on human nature. The experiment was called the United States.

In accordance with the promise that Manasseh would be a great nation, a civil war or rebellion, if you will, was launched by a motley minority of individuals who chose not to *belong* to the Crown or any state institution. This right to choose was called freedom and they died to keep it. The Author, as usual, saved the enterprise from being an abortion by the action of 5,000 years of accumulated wisdom in the person of Solomon, a Jew, who gave all of his fortune for the food and supplies which saved Washington's army.

The negative impact of ego-driven exploiters of the new republic was ameliorated by the expanse of the nation and its unlimited natural resources. A republic of sovereign states ceased to exist after a murderous civil war created the North American Union of State, one central absolute government of three tenuous hostile branches. After another hundred years, a progression of small incremental steps finally got God and supporters of the *mythological* figure out of the county by law. In 40 years of two generations, the experiment is essentially over and now the accumulated debt is called!

Preparing a nation for destruction means leading its people, by small incremental steps, to willfully corrupt themselves, which they do with marvelous ease. Hate and revenge are sophisticated appeals to the humanity of man, but the Angel has great success with the simple appeal of more, excess, and never enough. Excess in all things plays on the Angel's court. Food, drugs, sex, more goods, more land, more luxury, more adulation, more everything is insidiously innate in all people and promised to everyone subject to a surrender of choice. The promise of endless good and universal happiness in satisfying every desire may require trampling (killing a few for the betterment of all), especially when the ones trampled are not your kind.

In the past, wars were thought of as contests between gods, with humans as their surrogates in combat. There was usually a single ruler with lesser gods in support or opposition. This is helpful in understanding the key features of the war between the Author and the Angel, as well as the fate of those strange creatures: us!

The Author made a plan for our lives as individuals subject to our right of choice. By His choice, there were made unconditional promises to a genetic birthright people, the House of Jacob and the throne of David. It is evident that strategy and tactics will always be directed to invalidating at least one promise as they were from the beginning.

Most contemporary wars are won in their preparation. Destroying the lines of communication with God is a prime necessity. This requires time and control of programmed information by media and educational institutions to gradually indoctrinate the masses to accept that the governing elite represent God, if indeed there was a God. It is not only helpful, but necessary, to totally control children from birth so that the dependent object adopts all the ideology, hates, and loves of the institution to which it belongs. As the children move seamlessly from young mind control to school mind control, the mother is freed of home care and education. In this regard, home schooling is a criminal offense in some countries and merely regulated out of existence in others. For the children, the institution is mother, father, and god. Communication with family is gone, but so also responsibility. The institution is happy; the slave acolytes are happy; everything is happily under control. The system is so much more refined than the days Sparta raised all male children in an army of warriors and Turks stole Greek boys to be raised as an elite for the Sultan.

Now preparing for destruction and killing requires the setting of clear, realistic objectives, subject to the hope of the ultimate: World domination. All wars should be limited only to the objectives. This facet of warfare is best approached as a deadly chess game, not to be expanded to follow some abstract ideology.

As the senior member of the planning staff, I must *pray* that my intelligence agencies are temporarily at peace with one another and have broken off from domestic spying for at least a few minutes. With appropriate knowledge about the preparation and people who will be my opponents, I may anticipate the variety of moves that may be taken against our attack. All the while, we will stress the evil of our prospective opponent at the United Nations, while proclaiming our commitment to negotiation.

Now we strike! The cybernet is hit. We proceed with maximum speed to cause confusion and fear that makes the anticipated counter measure impossible and introduces emotional and uncoordinated responses that can be dealt with quickly and effectively. In this process it is ludicrous to suggest that broad moral regulation can be imposed. All morality resides in one person, the individual, who chooses and is responsible forever.

For clear examples of the efficacy of speed, look at the wars of the Mongols. Expanding population and drought on their plains caused them to take council for war. Employing their top weapons, the horse and the bow, they skimmed over lands at one hundred miles a day and butchered millions in a swath of destruction encompassing the jewels of Islam and Russia. They perfectly employed this principle of attack with its corollary: Terror. Long before their victim cities heard of their coming, they were in their midst. Guderian, Rommel, and Patton were quite good at this, using tanks and 85mm cannons instead of horses and arrows. Ruthless, but intelligent, the Mongols understood that unity of empire required ideology (religion) for the masses and adopted the state religion of Islam.

The most brilliant exponent of speed was certainly Alexander, who, possessed of supernatural power, was identified as a ram in motion subjecting all the nations of his time. His genius was to accept the gods of his conquered peoples, concentrating their collective power in himself. It is more than aside to mention that Constantine recognized the unifying strength of the Christian God and created a favored state religion about which he wedded the split Roman Empire into a ruling Byzantium.

A remarkable empire born supernaturally some 1,400 years ago is still with us in a fragmented state, but increasingly beginning to coalesce into a world class military force. Islam is remarkable in that it is not a state built about a religion, but an entity that is a state, religion, family, and individual, all in one. The sword of Islam speedily cut through the lands of Byzantium with a simple message: *submit or die.* It was launched against the world by the brilliant, but treacherous, Muawiya, from his base in Syria. Muawiya was proclaimed Khalifa in Jerusalem bringing about the Umayyad rule, paradoxically, a tribe much hated by the Prophet.

The complexity and pragmatic associations in any war were certainly exhibited in World War II. Atomic bombs were used to give the Japanese Emperor a rationale to surrender to the Americans; the Emperor having seen Stalin's policy worked out in Berlin. The Russian plan was to move from Manchuria to Hokkaido and the main island before the Americans. The northern islands of Japan would be the basis of an attack in Alaska at an expeditious time. All this was halted by the Japanese surrender and the threat of the use of atomic weapons against any significant action. All of this highlights the absolute need for sound intelligence monitoring your temporary friends and your temporary enemies.

Overriding all war since the cosmic day one is the person of God. His purpose and promises are well known and honest analysis, especially in retrospect, shows absolute consistency in the successful use of horror to deliver on His promise, in His way and His time. By God's choice, Hitler was an instrument in establishing Israel a nation in 1948. By God's choice, Stalin was an instrument in defeating the third German Empire and maintaining an equilibrium of terror before revolutionary nationalism and religious hatred introduced new alignments and tribalism.

In the war with God, the Angel is tenacious in using people to try to block any promise of God, for if he can negate one, he has destroyed them all. In this process, the often ignorant person selected by the Angel becomes a mortal enemy of God.

From the beginning, an objective of the Angel has been to adulterate the human gene pool and especially the genetic line of promise. This is the basis for the woman and her offspring being killed for bringing a threat to any of the irrevocable promises. Not surprisingly, people have extended the concept of adultery (women only) to be a genetic threat to family and tribe, punished by death.

An important (aren't they all?) eternal promise was given to David, that his line and the throne would rule over the House of Israel until God himself claimed it. With the stewardship of Jeremiah in joining the Davidic princesses to the ruling Zarehite kings of Spain and Ireland, we now find the succession complete in the genealogy of Queen Elizabeth who was annointed on that throne seated over Jacob's pillar. The Angel is brilliant in luring people, often completely ignorant of his plan, to thwart a promise of God. His plan was to bring a contender to the throne from the tribe of Esau; he failed, and three people were killed. There are none innocent in war when you have made God your enemy.

Now there is one most important rationale for war which is ideology; intellectual concepts, sometimes combined with religion, to embrace war as necessary for universal social justice. Their god is good, and any opposition will be destroyed, especially the individual and choice, which are the other God's chief interest. Paradoxically, a chief source of this pursuit for social justice lies in the centuries-old religious culture of the House of Jacob, the Jews. It always stands as a prime religious obligation to exhibit tolerance and work for treatment and opportunity, equal under just law.

It is useful to consider the plight of the Jews as a dispersed people who for 1,900 years had no functional homeland, were hated perpetual victims driven to near extinction by Islam and institutional Christianity; and yet they survived! The basis for their survival was the binding glue of religion and the preservation of the genetic unity of the tribe by strict historic rejection of adulteration. After the second century, Jews never considered military action as an option that was realistic for survival. From day one, they developed their intelligence to first seize any opportunity to be useful, and better, to be indispensable. Everyone was their enemy, but it was wise to choose the enemy that was most generous to their people. In this context for centuries after the death of Muhammad, the Jews were significant in Islamic governance and science, especially in Spain. The same can be said of philosophy, economics, and science in Christian Europe, especially in Poland, Holland, and later, England.

If an evolutionist was objective, it would be impressed by the genetic fact that is well understood by the Angel, viz., the way the brain responds to environmental parameters not only affects brain development, but is passed on in the genes. By keeping their children safe in the culture of education, science, philosophy, law, and a great religion, the Jews not only evaded, but infiltrated controlling institutions to the genetic advantage of their people. Thus, you see a superior people, crafted on one hand by isolation and on the other, waging a war in which their only weapon is their brain.

Born a Jew, Torquemada, as a convert to Catholicism, became the murderer of Jews as the Inquisitor General in Spain. This is the irony of fervent converts turning viciously on their own. In the last 200 years, an elite became converts to a system that dismissed or denied God as an agent in man's needs while framing their cultural social objectives in a form best represented by Engels and Marx. The promise of their thesis was very appealing to the intellectual Jew with the acceptance of revolutionary and military means for the good ends of an enslaved mankind.

For this brilliant minority, it is absolutely necessary to choose rightly whom and what to trust, for error is fatal. Napoleon was very attractive to European Jews in espousing some similar ideas of freedom by military means. English Jews, fully supportive of the ideology, chose British law and a growing recognition of Jewish talents as a better deal than the promise, but evident chaos of a Napoleon.

A recurrent suicidal bent was apparent in some choices made. Total commitment to the seduction of a classic scientific and philosophic milieu in Germany ended in a monumental disaster. Following the formula for world government with universal justice, Jewish women and men were at the Soviet forefront with Lenin, until he had them removed from *shared* power by execution.

Now, not only Jews, but many nations have turned from clumsy communism to very sophisticated pragmatic definitions of social reform, using modern technology to divorce individuality and choice from the person and put in place the god of government, with an elite to decide the best for the masses.

In the United States, the people did something potentially suicidal, viz., they replaced God with goddess in 1973, and for two generations of 40 years, proceeded to eliminate both physical and virtual signs of that *mythological* figure, replacing His teaching with the now state religion: evolution. Thus, having dismantled the historic defensive shield of America, the Angel could nudge the compliant animal *gods* toward their destruction by their external enemies.

The Author's list of lethal external enemies must start with Islam; followed by China, and a German led Europe. Islam will not stop in pursuing its destiny as a world-ruling force, albeit it will often find common interests with the other entities.

Unlike the Author and the Angel, the writer is human, with all the failings in interpreting the significance of events that are shaped by these supernatural personalities. I understand that the destruction of two buildings in New York fulfilled the Islamic requirement to warn the enemy of what is to come if it does not submit and accept the offer to convert as a nation to Islam. For my part, I did not understand why the Angel would permit his acolytes to warn the enemy of its intent by an action of no immediate advantage. As always, it is easy to see the brilliance of the supernatural contestants in retrospect. Indeed, the cost to Americans is immense and climbing: two lost wars claiming the lives of my best to no ends. Billions are spent on a ludicrous bureaucracy to accomplish the goal of the Angel with stupid brilliance. Individuals have been formed into compliant animal appendages of the institution by forced compliance to humiliation and abuse, while in fear that protest will be punished; not bad for a couple of buildings.

By now, you should wonder at a person or institution speaking of peace; a cessation of hostility. Well, scientifically and practically, that is achievable only in death.

Perhaps it is in this regard that a Muslim would speak of Islam as a peaceful religion. If you wish to pursue the idea of peace in Islam, consider its greatest and most revered mystic: al-Hallaj (Husayn il-Mansur - the Persian) who sought the only peace attainable on earth: union with God. About the year 914 AD, he received the Khalifa's version of peace by being crucified in Bagdad

In any religion, you can create truth by lifting what you wish from its context and ignoring all else. It is certainly possible that you may come to truly believe in your constructed truth. In Islam, there is the Prophet-inspired technique of taqiyya, wherein your position in an enemy state is such that it is expedient to lie and claim devotion to democracy, law, social justice, etc., anything that works to convince the enemy that there is a *moderate* position to be supported.

To the umma of Islam, the United States is their mortal enemy; a pagan, blasphemous people using every method of communication to spread their poisonous lifestyle and have the world adopt that evil. Their existence supports the Jews enslaving Arabs in stolen lands. The removal of this deadly obstacle to the global conversion and unity of Islam is not to be accomplished by terrorist attacks of a few adherents, but rather a single decisive blow that ends the power of this evil forever, the total destruction of the city of New York, the heart and brain of the Great Satan!

Picture the consequences of a truly effective strike: Five million killed, one million Jews killed, twenty trillion in financial loss as a starter, all in a matter of minutes. All of this is just a prelude to the chaos that follows. The economy of the country will be shattered as that of much of the rest of the world. The social fabric of the country will be ripped to hell with mobs satisfying their hate with acts of racial revenge.

It appears simple, needing only three things: a cargo ship (under any flag), one or more nuclear devices, and good technicians for assembly. The cargo ship, a container vessel, will have a large lead-lined sealed chamber in the hold covered with appropriate cargo. There are many nuclear bombs in the hands of Islamic entities, and others very hostile to the nation. Since there is no space limitation, technicians with expertise can assemble a hydrogen bomb if they wish. Once assembled, the room is sealed, camouflaged with cargo, and the ship sails on, until one day it brings its cargo to New York. The cargo is off-loaded, technicians come on board, unseal the space, activate the device, and leave. This process is not as novel as Tesla's electromagnetic pulse, but more psychologically devastating.

There is one problem, however: all this is impossible! Every step can be known in some part by the intelligence services of many nations besides the United States. The myriad of contributors to the venture will accidentally or deliberately disclose some part. In the face of many sources, the analysts of the abundance of data would have to be totally blind and deaf, precisely so!

Only two persons exist with the power to cloud the brains and senses of the women and men whom you trust to protect the nation: the Angel and the deposed God. Having dispensed with the myth of God as the protector of the nation, the elite crop of goddesses and gods, replace God with themselves and rejoice in the realm of the Angel. Brilliant women and men, clearly superior beings, driving mankind into a worldwide herd, have bought the lie of the Angel as from the beginning. The Angel's gods have chosen, and with their ideological fire, will do all described, unless the Author interferes. But He doesn't exist, does He?

As for us, the individuals stripped naked by technology and hunted as dangerous animals, there is our contract with the Author, whose power is forever greater than any on Earth. It will always be our right to choose the right and a loyal remnant will be the promised victor.

Origins — What and Who You Are

Having gone this far in the book, the reader and the writer can view themselves as survivors of a tortuous course of genocide and worldwide catastrophes. But more than that, you are an individual person, absolutely unique with no equal before you or after you and changing with the continuous motion of the Continuum. As a person, you share in the DNA commonality (but not equality) of humanity; something like the three Persons of a singular Godhead.

As a special creation, you are members of nothing, but everything is in you by that myriad of continuous choices that you make to cope with the shifting parameters of reality. Therefore, indeed, you are the family, the culture, the tribe, and obviously, the institution; all components of your discriminating choices. When these choices are right by your nature, you become beautifully engaged with the Creator of the Continuum by shared love and freedom.

To clearly understand the war into which you are born, look at the Hebrew Ten Commandments beyond trespass and sin and believe that it is the Author's design for what is right and true for the human individual's nature and his relation to all others in society. The Angel (super-pimp) has from the first lied to induce you to violate your nature by choosing to reject these strictures and bringing corruption and death to your being, separated from the life of the Author.

Consider that it is in the nature of animals to have the female bring progeny into the individual line, herd line, species line, etc. Whatever the environmental conditions require is instinctively sought out in the choice of the female, becoming genetically advantageous traits for survival. This system is so important that adulteration of the genome or individual genotype by the female will result in the killing of the intruder and the adulterous female. If this is true in nature, then what of the human species?

It is important to understand that the adulteration of the human genome was and is a prime objective of the Angel to create his version of humans. When he succeeded, his creation was destroyed by worldwide genocides. In this regard, we think of the myth-enshrouded high civilizations that were totally destroyed for having been corrupted by non-humans.

In the books of the Author, the importance of the woman bringing some kind of hybrid into the human genome is clearly a major issue between the Angel and God. God's perfect plan to guide a specific genetic line through history was almost thwarted by the sexual introduction of non-human elements in the seduction of supernatural agents of the Angel.

In searching out the contemporary history of human persons (viz. you readers), we need to appreciate that genetics and protection of certain lines from adulteration is a prime principle of the Author. We are chosen, multiplied families, descendant from the remnant survivors of old genocidal catastrophes. Thus, by genetic preference and survival instinct, you practice discrimination and prejudice daily on a primal level by your choices. To a major or minor degree, this applies to all human relations, your work, your play — everything. Your minor preferences change often, but social and institutional pressure is required to alter choice in ingrained preference. By nature, you are encouraged to stay and believe with your tribe.

If we stop thinking of sin to define adultery, homosexuality, divorce and pagan worship, and consider them as basic attacks on human genetics, then we can understand society's longtime treatment of these as capital crimes. As in Islamic states, the death penalty is still in force as this concept was permanently ingrained in family and tribal integrity. At present, Western nations regard the marriage contract of little significance in confirming and protecting genetic lines, with the possible exception in the lines of royalty. How the Author will choose in his response remains to be seen.

It is simple math to suggest that a current population of 7 billion originating from very few million some six thousand years ago, indicates that vast civilizations developed more than once in the 50,000 years of your existence, and were subject to practical extinction. Picture a continent like Australia located strategically over the mid-Atlantic rift, being an unstable plate surrounded by volcanic activity. Multiple volcanoes erupting below and above the sea borders of this plate caused the intervening land to collapse into the Atlantic in a matter of days, leaving only a few volcanic mountain peaks above the flood. Worthy of note is the relatively shallow Sargasso Sea which may cover a large remnant of the Atlantean continent.

In the many accounts of a great world flood, there has been included a *forty day rain* as an important contributing factor. If indeed there was widespread volcanic activity both in the sea and above, this continuous increase in water vapor plus volcanic micro-particles thrown to the clouds, would certainly create a multi-day cascade of frozen water crystals melting as rain.

Whether the flood just described is the one of historical oral and written record that is in all peoples of the earth is not clear. What is known is that the great dams at the Bosphorus and Gibraltar released a mile high Atlantic flood that turned placid Mediterranean and Black Sea lakes into raging seas, flooding millions of square miles and killing all life in its path. It is speculated that this event was some 6,700 years ago and significantly affected all of the then civilizations.

How these events occurred is speculative but, that great advanced civilizations thousands of years old were lost with only a remnant chosen to survive is fact. Except for the evidence of God's power in this issue, the reader and the writer would not exist.

If you can live with the fact that there were being superior in knowledge to the current human lot, then consider the exhibition of science that is largely preserved in stone to this day. Their unsurpassed accomplishments were in astronomy, mathematics and engineering; all clearly in the skeletal remains of that intellect. In South America, there is a strong oral history of the visitation of one or more *white* persons that came from the sea and taught skills and much else that was never to be learned any other way. All the impossible pyramids in those countries were altars of worship and sacrifice, but never tombs

At Giza in Egypt, two incomparable monuments, possibly 11,000 or more years old, are the Sphinx and the Great Pyramid, also called the Pillar of Enoch in the Egyptian Book of the Dead. The Sphinx identifies two figures of the zodiac: Virgo and Leo in an intimate relation between a virgin woman and a king. As for the Pyramid, it is an altar of witness containing with astonishing exactness in its construction, numbers which define the earth with a universal measure, including relationships in astronomy, mathematics, physics, engineering, and what else? It is not a tomb and contains no writing except some discredited graffiti. A stela indicates that the structure was worshipped by Khufu indicating prior existence, and with the Book of the Dead, a foreign origin for design and engineering beyond Pharonic ability.

It is prudent to establish our understanding of civilization as the content of everything that is the individual (you) and his works over generations. Development of civilizations prior to our time was constrained by the isolation of geography and obvious limits in communication. However, it is the living culture of these contained peoples that acts as the operative engine of their civilization. Shifting parameters of daily living will cumulatively cause the culture to progress, be relatively static or decline in a process of continuous change.

Cultures are generally viewed as embodied traditions, social conventions, idealized objectives; all bound and limited by regulation and law, ostensibly subscribed to by a majority. However, both on a tribal and individual basis, it is the inheritance of genetic traits that over time distinguishes and colors the civilization. Intellectually and physically, fear of the foreign as a threat to the integrity of a genetic group is an instinctive fact of life. So, also, preferential selection, prejudice, discrimination, intolerance and hatred are embedded in the human psyche, but the core life of culture and civilization is dependent on the unfettered choices of two individuals: you, the reader, and the Author. When you surrender your right to choose, you reject the Author and bring death to the family. Civilization thrives when it permits you, the individual, to fail and succeed in the pursuit of self-interest, while being tempered by law, human and supernatural, to restrict intentional harm to other individuals.

It is certainly true that historically, race was a significant, if not dominant, component of civilization. What in culture and civilization are races that flourish in the billions came about by choices made in genetic selection largely influenced by geography and often discriminatory isolation. Yet, if you were to suggest to the Chinese, Indian, Negro, Caucasian, etc., that each was an identifiable monolithic ethnic group, you might be called a fool in a number of languages. Asians know of a thousand ethnic types; Indians speak over a hundred different languages; Negroes vary in appearance and tribal loyalties over a continent; and Caucasians correctly describe a mountain range better than a people. Diversity reigns in humans as in no other creature because of individuality and choice.

You should not be surprised that your skin color played no significant role in your origins. You are a creature of shades of brown from creamy brown to purplish brown. There are no white people, for white is a reflection of all the rays of the solar spectrum, metaphorically associated with the sun god and the Author in the discourse of men and women. Black, on the other hand, is the absence of light and is fearfully associated with the evil of demons and, of course, the Angel. In our era of blatant ideology, either is used by the Angel to crucify by color; and it works!

The almost exclusive association of black with slavery is a gross historical demographic anomaly. Slaves have been an intrinsic social element in humanity since its beginning, chosen not by color, but qualifications for the needs and operation of the community. Israelites were slaves in Egypt, Persia, Assyria, Babylon and Rome, valued or abused based on their ability to be useful. As an aside, Jews kept slaves which were theoretically to be free in the fifty year Jubilee. Vikings provided Russian slaves by thousands for centuries to be sold to Arabs. Greek slaves also were valued for their intelligence for many centuries.

Slavery has always been a big business in which the Negro played a consistent, but minor, roll until sugar and cotton became the credibly most profitable agriculture commodities of the young industrial world.

Certainly, the Angel and his followers revel in the hate that can be produced by the irrelevant attribute of color. For the Author, an abstract consideration of color is ludicrous: What is it for you?

Reader, judge the elite that draw life from teaching their brothers and sisters to believe that they are genetic cripples, victims of an original sin of slavery, a hopeless mob that is self-destructive, feeding on revenge and hate. Do you then glory in watching your brothers and sisters eat their young?

By now, the reader's understanding of history is not *his story* but indeed your story. It is an often poetic rendition of the genetic trip of individual human survivors in a continuous intimate relationship with the Author. Certainly, the oral and written records of Egypt, Sumer (Iraq) and Greece are marvelous accounts of the people and times. However, bear in mind that the stories are of real people that migrated and flourished to raise up civilizations and dominate the world. Renamed and deified in heroic and re-ligious terms, they effectively enhance the greatest of all history books — the Author's Bible.

The Author's destruction of ancient civilizations that adulterated his human genome left the minimum family or tribe, chosen not for their *goodness*, but for their genetic integrity. All of the science and knowledge was retained to create an elite family to rule over the survivors. In this process, we benefit greatly in the move from oral recitation of reality to the written word with named personages and an understanding of what underlies myths. These records identify and follow the dispersed family some 7-10,000 years ago to establish the commonality of familial genetic origin of our present Asian, Indian, Negro and Shemetic peoples. While the communication and connections to God are enmeshed in myth and pagan worship by careful intent, the residual knowledge of the past plus the intellectual energy of the people caused great civilizations to rise and fall within the limits of geography and natural isolation.

Now appreciate that it is Egypt, the early cradle of Shemetic civilization, that has been central in the genetic line of humanity, carefully preserved through one or more genocides that moderns would call ethnic cleansing. Most of your post-flood history is embedded in the religious myths of Egypt and Iraq. In the account by the Author, Cush and Mizraim are descendent from Ham; Mizraim having drained the immense swamp that was lower Egypt and established that country as a Mediterranean food source for thousands of years. At this time, we encounter the story that was carried through the ages with name change and embellishment. It was Seth (Set), the shepherd king of upper Egypt, that fought and killed Osiris, the King of lower Egypt, while an identical story named Nimrod as the victim.

Osiris was identified with the sun god, and following his ritual death, his wife, now becoming the goddess Isis, was impregnated by a residual body part of Osiris, resulting in the birth of the reincarnated Osiris as the child god Horus. Nimrod, the son of Cush, has a similar course with Semiramis; his surviving wife being impregnated by a sunbeam giving us the virgin birth of Tammuz as the incarnate sun god. To the present, the Negro queens have been worshipped as the virgin goddesses who, through their choice, conceived the sun god on earth. If you doubt the thousands of years of influence on civilization and the human psyche, look at the names on our Hebrew calendar and the power of goddess worship in our time. A broad aside about these stories is that Egypt was, is, and will be a critical factor in our lives and the actions of empires and nations.

It is at this time that the Author chose a person and his genetic line to execute his plan for all peoples and all times. By physically entwining himself in the genetic line, he placed the seal of Divinity on the promise, and by his flesh and blood, he was the eternal guarantor for those that choose life.

By association with Shem, Abram was able to retrieve a relationship with the one God from a morass of gods and goddesses. Now called Abraham, his detailed genetic record is enfolded into the core of the Author's history book — the Bible. If you are familiar with the phrase "one man and one woman," then know that the one man, Abram, was a Hittite that had his name changed to Abraham, becoming grandfather for some three billion grandchildren now living. A beautiful, fair-skinned Aramean or

Hittite woman named Sarah by the Author is correspondingly your grandmother. In over 4,000 years, this chosen line was the voice of the Author, taking his promise to every race and nation. Thus, in the face of eternal hatred of the Angel and the vagaries of trillions of individual choices, the Author proves himself God.

Of the two Abrahamic lines we first address, the collateral line originated in Ismael, a son by the Egyptian woman, Hagar, to which was added the tribe of Ibrahim's grandson, Esau. These lines for 40 centuries have constituted the great Arab tribes. Now these people are engaged in a final resolution to their history under the rule of Islam.

Now we will engage the eternally appointed royal line of Abraham in his son, Isaac, and grandson, Jacob, renamed Israel, accurately detailed in the books of the Bible. It is clear that the Author required of all 13 tribes of Israel to experience both trial and conditioning for several centuries in the civilization of Egypt before they set forth to establish the world civilization that we now possess. It is Joseph, sold as a slave into Egypt, who some ten years later became the sole operating head of the Egyptian bureaucracy answerable only to Pharaoh. In that capacity, he brought his father and the entire 11 tribes of Israel from Canaan, giving them the best lands of Egypt. He established absolute rule with his family over all Egyptians as the historic Hyksos, the self-identified *shepherd kings*!

Contemplate the incomparable perfect execution of the Author's plan for the children of Abraham becoming nations and possessing the world. By being immersed for four centuries in the greatest civilization of all time, the Israelites incorporated Egyptian DNA and with it, the thousands of years of science and knowledge that they used to establish Greek and Western civilization. Making full use of their intelligence, these people developed advanced technology of war in the use of the horse and chariot, as well as the bow. Their consistent love for the horse survives in the skill of their Irish progeny.

For the sake of simplicity, we define genetic events as birth and life or death and extinction. With that, the Author directed two genetic events that initiated historical drama over thousands of years and are clearly unknown to so-called scholars. The daughter of the high priest of Egypt gave birth to Manasseh and Ephraim, sons of Joseph, to become powers in the house of Israel, rivaling

Judah to give us the American experiment and the British Empire of nations. By addition of the two tribes of Joseph, the House of Israel now was 13 tribes in number. Note: The House of Joseph in no way challenged Judah as the eternal possessor of the scepter and law which was then passed to first born males

At this juncture, it is logical to introduce the historic time line for the people and events of our Egyptian beginnings:

1868 B.C.	Joseph into Egypt as a slave
1843 B.C.	Jacob to Egypt as king from Canaan
1826 B.C.	Jacob dies
1772 B.C.	Joseph dies
1760 B.C.	All the tribes are called by Hyksos (shepherd kings)
1580 B.C.	Exodus of Hyksos leaders led by Zarehites
1527 B.C.	Moses born — now slaves
1453 B.C.	The Exodus — Phares line with 13 tribes

It will become evident that all 13 tribes dominated the development of the nations of the West and are visible in the heraldic standards that identified each tribe since leaving Egypt. However, the two genetic lines of Judah hold the pre-eminent position, as will be shown. With some intrigue on the part of the Author, Tamar became wife of Judah and gave birth to twin boys, Zareh and Phares. The first born was Zareh, and he was marked with a scarlet thread to indicate his primacy, which is attested to by our rampant red lion signifying the right of Kingship.

With Joseph gone and the advent of second and third generation Israelites led by Judah and then by the Zarehites, the name Hyksos (shepherd kings) was applied to these rules who developed the horse, chariot, compound bow and battle axe used with great skill for 2,000 years. Their rule was forcefully contested by the Pharaohs of upper Egypt. Kamose, whose father was killed in an early revolt, followed up with more success, but it was his brother, Ahmose, who took Sharuhen, the key Hyksos ancestral base in Canaan. By 1576 B.C., the residential Hyksos were a generation of slaves.

We will take temporary leave of the Phares line to pursue the historic course of the sons of Zareh. In no way does this deny the cosmic importance of the Phares genetic line that includes the life and presence of the Author. Certainly the many generations of the tribes pursued every opportunity to profit from war and exploration of their world. The ships of Dan roamed the Mediterranean coasts, Spain, France, and Ireland in which they established settlements. Being hated by Egyptians and threatened with total defeat by Ahmose, it was very prudent of the Zarehite rulers and other tribal leaders to take their leave of Egypt. Using the ships of Dan and the Phoenicians to leave with all of the treasure of Egypt, they embarked on a course that would shape Greek and Western civilization forever.

It is now the five sons of Zareh that brings up names familiar to the reader. Dardanus established Troy on the Turkish coast while the other brothers founded Athens, Sparta and further dominated the whole of the Iberian peninsula. It is likely that Benjamites accompanied Darda to Turkey. Bear in mind that *progress* is a process of competition, war, and often family rupture. Thus it is that the tribe breaks into elements with individuals seeking advantage in the shifting parameters of chaos.

Subsequent sons of the founders in the Greek-Turkey area conducted significant battles for Troy in which the Greeks were victorious. The Trojan leader, Aeneas, withdrew by sea, leaving much as the Zarehites had departed from Egypt. In his well-documented voyages, Aeneas and his Trojans established themselves as founders of Carthage, Sicily and Rome.

In the generations of their rule in Sicily, there was born the great grandson of Aeneas destined to impact Europe to this day; this was the famous Brutus. Exiled by the Trojans for having killed his father in a hunting accident, he went to the Greek lands. There, finding Trojans enslaved by the Greeks, he mobilized them and defeated the Greeks. In the peace agreement, Brutus gained a princess in marriage and many completely provisioned ships on which he took all the Trojan clans under his command.

Sailing to the Iberian Atlantic coast, they were well received by their ancestral kin and especially by one of the chiefs, Corineus. It is certain that Brutus knew of the lands that he was seeking from the accounts of generations of sailors going back to their time in Egypt. With the clans of Corineus, and probably Ephraim as well, Brutus came upon the south coast of Britain where Corineus established the kingdom of Cornwall while Brutus placed his people on the Thames, creating there New Troy while for the whole land, the Hebrew-based name Britain, meaning *covenant land*. As for the people, they now bore the name *Brit-ishi*, meaning a covenant people. So executes the Author his design and promise!

Now let us go back in time and space to our people in Egypt in the year 1527 BC, where we meet with Hatshepsut, a daughter of Thutmose I and Queen Amose. She had one daughter and a Levite child called Moses. When her husband, Thutmose II, died in 1512 BC, she became regent and in 1503 BC declared herself to be Pharaoh. Having married her daughter to Thutmose III and supporting Moses in the Egyptian military, this remarkable woman passed the rule of the land to Thutmose III at about 1490 BC, following which the 25-year-old ruler conducted campaigns in Canaan, reducing all the tribes and extracting regular tribute.

At some time during the reign of his stepmother, Moses fled from Egypt to save his life. Returning about 1460 BC, Moses wins the release of all the enslaved tribes in 1453 BC, at which time they exit with huge amounts of gold. In pursuit, Thutmose forces suffer significant losses and he dies in 1450 BC. Having been totally corrupted by their years in slavery, which they now preferred to freedom, that generation died in the desert. It was the next generation of 13 tribes that returned to Canaan in 1413 BC to establish themselves over the next 1000 years.

Now about 1000 BC, one of the line of Phares in the tribe of Judah was raised up king of the 13 tribes. This king, David, extended the tribal borders to their promised extent from the Euphrates to the Nile. To him, the Author vowed eternal kingship over the House of Israel, which is now had in the person of Queen Elizabeth. Upon the death of David's son, Solomon, the successor precipitated a revolution which separated the land of Judah and Jerusalem from the 11 tribes of the House of Israel in Samaria to the north. Thus was born the first named Jew as the House of Jacob, including the tribe of Benjamin by virtue of their right to Jerusalem. While Jews remained in their general area for another thousand years, the House of Israel, now under the rule of the Ephraimite Jeroboam, would within three generations be thrust into the western world to create our civilization as to the present.

About 960 BC, Assyria initiated a process of removal of each of the 11 tribes from their individual tribal areas in the northern kingdom and moving them to northern Persia to be a buffer against the Medes. By 721 BC, all of Israel was gone, with Sargon taking the last half tribe of Manasseh. However, by 720 BC, Simeon was in Wales and Danites in Spain and Ireland, effecting their escape by sea, using their extensive fleets of ships. All of the tribes maintained their integrity, although cooperation was common; there was no central authority of kings or priests. Assyria was not yet finished, for in 675 BC, it conquers Egypt and yet in 612 BC, Nineveh is destroyed by Scythians and Medes.

It was during this period that the tribes were given or adopted new generic names for individual or associated groups with the exception of Danites, which have their name on Denmark and many rivers across Europe. All tribes kept their identifying standards from 1400 BC to the present, so it is easy to locate them in the countries that they rule at present. It is instructive to observe that color-crazed ideologies have universally indicated that Caucasian means white persons, which indeed they were very fair-skinned, blue-eyed, with red and blonde hair inherited from Abraham and Sarah, and seen in every land in which the House of Israel dominates.

Consider that a million of 11 separate tribes were torn from their lands over a period of 200 years and lodged at the border of the Medes with no obvious resources beyond their fighting skills, intellect, and effective tribal bonds: yet in 300 years, they conquered the world. The principal component of that conquest was their disinterest in any urban development but rather choosing mobile booths and tents which caused them to be called wanderers, strangers and nomads from the Ukraine to Scotland. The other components were wise military choices including adopting the horse from Median cavalry and developing the trefoil arrowhead (iron), a recurved, laminated bow and the battle axe. All this worked well with the horse on the plains of eastern Europe.

Both the Persians and Greeks left to us some of the names by which we are known. In 450 BC, the historian Herodotus used the name Keltor-Celts as a generic for all the tribes. Another prominent group of Israelites developed ties with their long ago Greek kinsmen to effectively control the grain trade in 675 BC. The Greeks called them Scythians, meaning nomads. These *nomads* were special to history for by 610 BC, they were in the Ukraine following other Israelite tribes. In the period 600 to 300 BC, they extended their empire from south Siberia to the western Black Sea. Like their cousins, they established no significant settlements, but moved on relentlessly into Europe.

In 600 BC, the Germani Celts extended from Greece to Scandinavia, speaking a common language based on Hebrew. Gauthi, the sons of God (Goths) ranged from northern Germany, Holstein, Jutland and Russia. One group within the Goths were Teutons, a word meaning stranger. By 570 BC, several tribes filled Poland and divided it into upper and lower Moise (Moses) which still stands as greater and smaller Poland in this day. By 513 BC, they were in command of Thrace and Bulgaria as Celts.

In 870 BC, the King of Samaria was Khumri (Omri), so highly regarded that Persians described the translated Israelites as *bet Khumri* — sons of Khumri. Now you encounter Greek named Cimmerians, Cambrians in Germany, Kimri in Wales and Kimri in Crimea using a Hebraic speech preceding that of Solomon.

In 517 BC, yet another famous name originates in Darius's description of three tribes as socca, the sons of

Isaac, later to become Saxons. The same Darius has left us a picture of the tribes on the Behestun rock carving. There they are pictured as either slaves or subjects.

With Assyria gone, Chaldeans not only filled the void but attacked the land of Judea, imprisoned the royal household and moved all the Jews from their land to Babylon where many remained for centuries under subsequent Persian rule. It was in Babylon that Zedikiah, the Davidic head of the Phares line of Judah, was killed along with all of his sons, but not his two daughters. Of course, with the death of all the males of the royal house, it was clearly the end of the Author's *perpetual throne of David* — except — that absent males, the Mosaic law decrees that daughters are the genetic inheritors of the throne (DNA counts).

It was now that Jeremiah, the great grandfather of the princesses, fully understanding what the Author expected of him, moved quickly, taking the two women to the safety of a Greek colony of mercenaries in Egypt in 583 BC. The prophet returned to Jerusalem to secret the sacred objects of the Temple but taking with him Jacob's pillar, the stone on which Davidic royals were and are crowned up to the present.

Jeremiah and his scribe, Simon Baruch, next took ship conveying the princesses to Spain where one lady was wed to the Zarehite Melitian king. The other daughter, the famous Tea Tephi, was taken to Ireland, and there at Tara was joined to the Zareh line seated above Jacob's pillar. Thus the genetic lines of Judah, Phares and Zareh were united in the throne of David. Also at Tara was a school of Mosaic law established teaching principles of governance, which shaped ideas of law in Britain and the United States.

So now 2 billion people have read of their genetic history over a period of 4,000 years as also the world has been introduced to the 11 tribes of the House of Israel. For 2,000 years, the House of Jacob has known and preserved its genetic identity and nowhere in the world are they not known as Jews. As has been shown, the line of David involves kingship as no other on earth.

Your genetic story now explodes by an event that shook the Continuum and caused a virtual halt in the motion of the universe. It was the moment when our Author set aside his divinity to engage humanity as your kinsman by inserting himself physically into your DNA stream as a child born in 2 BC and proceeded to represent in himself kin to every human alive, dead, or yet to live. Completing his mission for the peoples of the world, he is seated on his throne in the Continuum by right until he chooses to add the earthly throne of David by right. In this way, the genetic history of humanity concludes.

Christianity

Christianity is the explanation of creation and God's plan for humanity; violated by our first genetic kin, then salvaged and restored by the blood of Jesus the Christ, Son of God, which will end by the will of God to be translated into its fulfillment in eternity. The first humans, Adam and Eve, were conceived immaculate as were the prior spirit beings, one third of whom used their right of free choice to rebel against God led by the beautiful and brilliant Lucifer, self-proclaimed Angel of Light. So it was that the human was created, a body and spirit with a soul, gifted with choice, set to live forever in love with God, subject to a covenant of obedience which, if violated, would cause them to die.

It is unlikely that the new creations understood the existent ancient war between God and the rebel Angel, Lucifer. Thus it was that the woman was beguiled by his beauty and skill with words to portray a lie as truth and truth subject to interpretation. The woman was convinced and acted on the promise of the Angel that she would be like God, a goddess. Adam accepted the lie and joined in the fatal choice to disobey — sin!

By now, the reader should understand that personal responsibility is intrinsic in the absolute right of choice. All are in an unrelenting war and under a curse specific in that all are now born dead in sin, a grafting of inherited disobedience in our spiritual DNA. Hence, the Baptism ritual, as well as all sacraments have the individual choose to endure a virtual death to sin and be reborn resurrected. All sacraments are dead rituals except for the life that the individual brings to them. Christianity is totally personal.

For 2,000 years, temporary stays in God's judgment on humanity was had by the blood offering of unblemished animals. Association with blood is no accident since it is accepted that the life of the soul is in the blood. Thus the blood of one animal was to stay the punishment of all the brethren. It was made clear that the individual could do nothing that was adequate to satisfy God's justice, but in the wealth of his love for mankind, God speaking through his prophets described in detail the perfect person that he would send to be kin to all humanity and by his proscribed death by crucifixion and resurrection return to the Father to be accepted as adequate atonement for all sin that was placed on him. Now it is possible to choose life by belief and worship of the Christ in mutual complete love.

God is consistent in his love for each individual person so as to have placed something like a spirit cell in our human make-up with receptors for hearing and responding to what is called *the grace of God.* The army of agents of the Angel are skilled and successful in blocking your receptors with an accumulation of every imaginable deviation from truth as once again you believe the great liar and murderer. A Christian must achieve and maintain a state of Amen in which you are always open to the presence of the Holy Spirit of whom Jesus said, "You will not approach the Father except the Holy Spirit draw you." So it is that the Christian engages all three persons of the Trinity in an embrace of total love and eternal life.

To approach understanding the Trinity, three persons in the oneness nature of God, consider that you are an individual person sharing a single factual nature with every other human person. In the god-head, the Father, Jesus the Son, and the Holy Spirit share a single divine nature, but as in humans, they express that nature in unique and different ways. Love, however, is a co-existent attribute of the Trinity which in salvaging the cursed nature of man required the crucifixion of Jesus to satisfy perfectly God's justice. This gives us a choice of life in the grace of God (a gift) or hate and death in the offering of the Angel that dominates the earth.

Christianity is both simple and cosmic in that you render all aspects of your being in love to Jesus Christ — God. Remember that Jesus said that you must be open to the Holy Spirit to be drawn to the Father. After his death and resurrection, Jesus is the power to forgive sin and makes it clear that, "no one comes to the Father but through me"!

Jesus' commandments are based on love; they are simple but profound: *You are to love God with your whole being and your neighbor as ourself.* He requires water baptism to cleanse a person to permit the Holy Spirit to do his work (also baptism of the Holy Spirit).

Jesus established a daily offering and sacrifice in the Eucharist in which both bread and wine necessary for physical life convey spiritual life when taken with the Christ — real communion with God. Consider how the Christian may encounter the Christ each morning:

Jesus, bless the bread and wine which I now take, and bless me, that these all are holy offerings. As I take of these, I witness and declare before the Father and Heaven that your covenant is fulfilled in me. I have taken of your flesh and blood: your healing, your strength, your life and soul. Anointed by you, a priest, I gave my body and blood at the tree. Now my body and soul are in your forever. I do this now (take the bread and wine) before the Father and Heaven with my love, my trust, and my thanks!

This act of witness and affirmation will nourish you with the leaven of love in the bread and the wine, a witness that your sins borne by the Christ, are washed away forever by His blood.

Jeshua — the Christ

In the fullness of time, a king was born to a virgin, Meriam, of the House of David in the Hebrew new year, September, 2 BC. For 1500 years, the Torah and the Prophets told in exquisite detail of the life, death, and purpose of a Messiah that would redeem the House of Jacob and all Israel. This man was to be their kinsman not only to the Jew but to every human being. In his life and death he fulfilled the law in every regard

The Passover in Egypt was the first Eucharist, a dramatic metaphor for the Messiah's death and purpose. A perfect male lamb was kept in each house for three days, sacrificed on the chosen day and hour, flesh eaten for healing and strength while the blood was placed on every Israelite door lintel and the two side posts. It was the blood of innocence that preserved Israel from the death visited upon Egypt. And God stayed with his people telling them in many ways and in incomparable detail of him that was to come.

"You are without excuse!"

A child called *God with us* was miraculously conceived by the power of the Holy Ghost in the womb of Miriam. She, being active in the Faith in the state of Amen, open to be *full of grace*, chose to *let it be done*. In that moment, God formed the promised redeemer, his son Jesus, with a fully human but sinless nature. With her blood nourishing the child, there must have been a sharing of life and souls in a relation which we may know more deeply in communion with the risen Christ in the Eucharist.

Jesus was born six months after the birth of John the Baptist in September of 2 BC, on the first day of the Hebrew new year. His birth was marked by astronomical events that caused three mystics to drive their caravans for hundreds of miles to worship the King of the Jews some one year after his birth. They came from a land where centuries before Daniel spoke of the Lord's coming and the story was not lost.

Not much more is written of the Christ for some time for two obvious reasons: his public *three years* had not yet come and his writers were years in the future. One reported event was Jesus having a learned discourse with the sages in the Temple at the age of 12. The impossibility of a child to be permitted such access introduces us to

Joseph of Aramathea. Joseph was Miriam's uncle, a power in the Sanhedrin and in control of the tin trade for the Roman Empire. It is clear that Joseph was deeply involved in the life of Jesus for as long as Miriam, and was to be a key person in the Christianity of Britain and France as we shall see. This relationship was to facilitate the disappearance of Jesus from Judea using Joseph's trade route to the Cornwall mines in England where he stayed until about 29 years of age. He then returned to begin his three years of showing himself as the fulfillment of the law and prophets.

In Judea at that time, John the Baptist was a universally known and respected prophet and yet did not recognize the stranger who had just paid the Roman tax on newcomers to Judea. It is clear that Jesus had grown to manhood in isolation from family and friends. With the baptism of Jesus by John on October 14 in 29 AD and the descent of the Holy Spirit upon Jesus, there began the three years of his public ministry to the Jews.

In the years that followed, Jesus gathered a band of 12 men to be called his apostles, and many acolytes that were convinced of his special calling, especially in the many physical miracles that he performed in the sight of many. It was when he forgave sins that he drew calls of blasphemy from the priests and Pharisees. Then as now, Rome desired religious leaders to keep the people content with their role as servants of the state and keep taxes flo - ing. The elite of the Jews were more than ready to cooperate, even at the sacrifice of life — of others of course!

Thus, after thousands of years, it was April of the year 32 AD that was set by the Father for Christ to exactly fulfill the set times (feast days) of the Jewish religious new year. In the fulfillment of prophecy, there are no accidents. The year chosen had to be the year in which the three holy days would occur exactly as they did. Sundown marks the beginning of a new Hebrew day, so on your gentile calendar, Tuesday night began Wednesday, the day on which the perfect male lambs are killed in the Temple at exactly 3 p.m., blood drawn and offered for the sins of the people by the High Priest. So it was on that Tuesday night that Jesus and his 12 apostles sat for the Passover meal, the first of the set times of the Lord and the day that would shake the Continuum with the offering of eternity with God to every human that ever existed. A universe uniquely shaped by the Word to support our life trembled at the death and resurrection of its Maker and in that moment was opened to us as a shared possession with God.

It is important to imagine how Jesus, the Son of God, always had full knowledge of every act of torture that He would suffer and the weight of all the sins of mankind placed upon Him unto death. Also consider that He had always, by right, the opportunity to reject the horror; he had to grant his free consent.

Jesus blessed the bread and wine, ate and drank with others, having declared the bread was a symbol of His body torn, that they might have true physical and spiritual food and healing as he bore all infirmitie in his body. In the Passover tradition, the third wine cup was silver to stand for the removal of sin from the partaker. It is at the blessing of this cup that Jesus stated that his blood would be shed for many. How much the apostles, including Judas, understood of what they experienced is limited by the fact that the Holy Spirit had not yet fully possessed them, as later He would.

After years of nourishing hatred and fear of this Jesus, the priests, scribes and elite of the Sanhedrin were seriously planning to get the Roman authority to kill the *pretender*, king of the Jews. There was comfort in saying that one should die rather a nation perish (along with their jobs and income). After his betrayal to the well-paid mob of Jews, he was taken to the High Priest, accused of blasphemy, and taken to Pilate, who alone had the power for execution in Judea. Pilate wisely deferred to Herod who sent him again to Pilate. There at early dawn, Jesus presented himself as king of the Jews and offering no defense to stay what must happen. As was the Passover custom, Pilate offered the mob to free Jesus or a notorious murderer. They chose Barabbas, the murderer!

What followed from the ninth hour on Wednesday morning was for the Romans a fun-filled torture of an *insane* Jew. He was whipped until his back and shoulder muscles were shredded. A crown of thorns was embedded into his head amid much comic saluting of this king. For his close supporters, there was sheer agony and horror and real confusion that this is happening to the Son of God.

It was now near the twelfth hour and time to take Jesus to the *main event*. At Jerusalem, a tree was routinely used with a slot cut for placement of a six foot beam and a wooden footrest fixed in place. Jesus was to carry the beam to the tree, but having no functional muscles, he couldn't handle the weight. Having collapsed and dropped the beam, the soldiers seized upon the nearest male Jew to carry the beam and get moving. Having done hundreds of crucifixions, they proceeded: two to tie and nail, four to lift into the slot and then feet nailed to the support to extend the life and suffering. As required by law, a sign was placed on the tree above the head of Jesus with his crime described in three languages: *King of the Jews*. It was the twelfth hour. In strict observance of the law, the priests in the Temple begin killing the lambs of the Passover sacrifice at exactly three in the afternoon. On the tree, the perfect sacrifice of the Eucharist was complete — Jesus was dead! Nature was quiet for a moment and then shook as the whole cosmos responded and changed for eternity.

Routinely, the criminal's naked body was taken down and dumped just outside the city to be a feast for wild dogs and rats while the nails and beam were put aside for future use. Joseph of Arimathea, as a family member of Jesus and a power in Roman commerce, required of Pilate that he be given the body. Pilate needed to verify that Jesus was really dead in the remarkably short time period, but then, having done so, he granted the release. Joseph had a rock-hewn tomb which he had prepared for himself, but now his men placed the body on a slab in the tomb, and after using some embalming compound, the body was wrapped in fine linen cloth and a stone was rolled over the entrance to keep animals out. All this needed to be done before the eve of the next day, which was a sabbath. On Friday, when the shops were open, the women went to buy spices to further anoint the body. Again as the eve brought a Saturday sabbath, they waited until evening, and on Sunday morning went to the tomb. A Roman seal, placed on the stone, and a Jewish guard were to ensure that Christ rising on the third day was not to be staged. At some time after the three days and three nights, Jesus rose from the dead, resurrected by the Father, passed through the linen cloth, and through the rock closing the tomb, causing the guards to flee in terror. In this he fulfilled the holy day of First Fruits.

When the women arrived, the stone had been rolled away for them to see the empty tomb. An angelic person at the entrance explained that Jesus was risen and was to appear to many who still doubted their senses. One final act was necessary to complete this Eucharist. Before being touched, Jesus had to present himself to the Father as a blood offering. The sacrifice accepted by the Father completed all in perfect justice.

The future is now present and as he came in peace as a servant, he now comes as king to end a very long war.

The Institution

Jesus now restored to the kingship at the right hand of the Father has by his blood won very simple choices and instructions for all humanity. The Christian believes that Jesus is man and God and is to be worshipped as such with the total love of the individual poured out upon God and neighbor kin in Christ. As your love flows out, it is continually replenished by the Christ in a never-ending cycle of life. The Eucharist celebrates Christ's Passover and the individual's witness of personal offering of self then being resurrected in body and spirit. Although there is no evidence of all of the acolytes being Christian baptized, there was an instruction to baptize all nations taken to mean *of water* but accepting baptism of spirit. That was it; a family of individuals with God.

In 35 AD, Joseph of Arimathea took this fundamental conceptual Christianity to Marseille with Lazarus, Magda, Martha and possibly Miriam. In 36 AD or 38 AD, Joseph went to Britain followed by Simon the Zealot, Aristobulus (first bishop of Britain), then Paul in 56-58 AD. At Glastonbury, the first Christian Church had been easy to establish with the memory of Christ's long stay still fresh. With the marriage of Joseph's daughter, Anna, to a prince of the House of Israel, there was wedded Christianity, the House of David, and a future royal line in Britain. Not surprising was the rejection of Augustine and the Roman Church in a power grab. However, by 606 AD, Rome effectively displaced the Brits for supremacy.

In the reign of emperor Claudius, events led to the establishment of the second Christian church, that of the British at Rome. Theradox, a respected British king, was fighting the Romans when he was taken and in Rome gave an impressive speech for freedom to the Senate which preserved his life but required his stay in Rome. His wife, a Christian, was mother to Gladys, later renamed Claudia, also a Christian. A religious connection is centered on the senator Rufus Pudens being the step-brother of the apostle Paul in their Christian mother, Saint Priscilla. A son, Linus, was the first bishop of the British Roman Church. Of this family, all but Claudia were murdered by the government and that congregation was all terminated by 140 AD. Using his brother's family as a base in Rome in 57 AD, Paul spent some eight years following the path of Danites and Zarehites through Gaul, Spain and Britain. In 66 AD, Paul's body may have been taken by Claudia's family, thus ending a chapter of remarkable simplicity and beauty.

Magdalin College at Oxford has three fragments of Matthew's 26th chapter certified as written in Antioch mid first century. Knowing that Mark writing in Alexandria preceded Matthew, we can speculate that both Gospels were in circulation in the first twenty years following the death of Jesus.

With James and Peter in charge at Jerusalem, this somewhat chaotic Christianity was 100% Jewish in its apostles, membership and structure, requiring that you become a Jew first with the Christ added. It was Matthew writing to the Jew and Mark to the gentile that stimulated discussion, if not unity. After spending three years with the person of the risen Christ, Paul brought truth and clarity to the synagogues of many communities often to the hostility of the entrenched hierarchy. The *infallible* leaders never accepted gentiles or indeed understood who was the Christ. In the *service* of God, they stoned Stephen for rejecting Jewish ritual and professing the simple truth of Jesus.

In the year 70 AD, the Romans ended a revolt in Jerusalem by killing thousands of Jews and utterly destroying the Temple, thus ending the Jewish bishopric in Jerusalem leaving Antioch, Alexandria and Rome as competing sees. A last vigorous revolt of Jews against Rome was led by Jesus-hater Simon bar Kokhba over the years 132-135 AD, resulting in the slaughter of half a million Jews and a final break between synagogue and church. Now the Jews were left to reinvent themselves, and so they did.

By 165 AD, there were 20 Christian sects with the bishops of the three sees and their elite adherents competing for power and leadership. These early institutions did not create their absolute control on an individual's faith action of love based on belief in Jesus, the Son of God, or on Paul's holding that it is what the individual brings to the Eucharist that determines its validity. But there was an item of unity supported by saints, Fathers of the Church, Augustine and Aquinas up to our present. It was the emotional excitement of hating and contempt for the Jews, excluding them from being fully human and killing them in the *service of God*. Hate is the stink that draws legions of powerful demons who hold seats in the councils of these developing institutions to the present.

Pauline baptism was a ritual symbolic of real dying and rising in the Christ. It was done naked as Christ was naked with three immersions, as Christ was three days in the grave. Post Paul and the apostles, it became a sacrament of exorcism. In North Africa, baptism held no regard for Christ and the apostles were not baptized. Tertullian held that an angel made the water holy with healing properties, but rejected child baptism. Origin accepted child baptism but indicated only prior sins were forgiven (better delay!). John held that the water was the effective agent not symbolic, so when the bishop blesses the water, the Holy Spirit is captured in the water and the body becomes holy resurrected flesh with the remission of sins. Hermes held baptism absolutely necessary for salvation by resurrecting the body to make it eternal. Whatever the views, the claimed absolute is that the Church is the dispenser of salvation.

Jesus also made the keeping of the Eucharist a principle of daily observance by command to his apostles. These apostles had a daily Eucharist until the Christ resurrected appeared and ate with them. Obviously he was the

Eucharist to be served in *memory* forever until you too ate and drank with the Christ at the end of the age. Among the contenders, Tertullian had the Spirit entering into the bread and wine causing the body to become immortal. Iraneus postulated no transubstantiation but the bread and wine become a vehicle of the Logos Spirit united with the natural product. For Justinian, it was simply food for the body and life for the soul. Ignatius held that the ritual made flesh divine. Note that emphasis was always bread and bodily immortality with wine secondary as often replaced with water and rarely offered to the laity except logically at Easter (Passover). It took 800 years to move the Eucharist from the home to the Basilica where the institution created a form of sacrifice in which the priest brought the Christ into the elements and then he consumed the body and blood. Thus once again, only the Church could summon God to a table (altar) in the service of the people.

At this time, the concern of individual Christians was systematic persecution for refusing to worship the many state gods of Rome much the same in a different context today. In the third century, Decius, Valerian and Diocletian were aggressive murderers of Christians until the son of a British Christian mother won command of the Empire setting his seat at Byzantium, later named Constantinople. This was the great Constantine who understood the unity that comes from a single religion bonded to the state, took advantage of the extent of Christianity in his army to declare his receipt of a vision from their God for whom he was to fight and establish a Christian Roman Empire. In short order, from the year 312 AD, pagans were killed, their temples and shrines turned into church buildings, cults outlawed and looted, and gnostics especially hard hit as anti-establishment. Now the two institutions, government and Church, are wedded while engaged also in a perpetual struggle for dominance.

Constantine now took notice of a significant cause for disorder in his Church viz exactly who or what was Jesus Christ (more properly — who is?). Tertullian accepting only the four gospels would cite the Logos of John always divine. In the mix, some believed him an angel or created and then adopted by the Father. Arius of Alexandria proposed that he was not of the same nature as God. He was branded a heretic but never recanted. In another thesis, Jesus was two persons; a man that died and God.

Under the guise of addressing the question of Miriam being the mother of God, the real question of who exactly is Jesus was called to be resolved by Constantine in a council of all the sees at Nicea in 325 AD. The power alignments between Alexandria, Rome and Constantinople under pressure from Constantine for a consensus resulted in a ban on Arius and the Arian position. Nicea determined and declared Jesus is one person with a human nature and a divine nature, man and God, the human nature created by the Holy Spirit at a set time using Miriam as a vehicle for the body with the divine nature set aside but always there in the one person. God does not have a mother.

Despising Jews did not at all deter the Corporation from adapting and Christianizing most of Judaism's structural elements. The high priest was now pope; the Sanhedrin becomes the College of Cardinals, priests and Levites become priests and bishops, and there was now a church-temple for the Mass ritual, with an altar at which sacrifice was made and the body and blood consumed by the priest. Also a barrier, often of icons, was in place to seal off the Holy of Holies from the laity.

The Angel of Light — Satan — in his war with God,

makes every effort to kill every Jew existent and thus mock God's promises to the House of Jacob. A second goal is to control religion, especially in concert with secular government. In all cases, it is power and control that completely effaces the individual and his God. His success rate is over 90%.

In the next 300 years after Constantine, the three sees developed as indicated in an otherwise pagan world. Arianism still remained an important belief, especially in areas in the periphery of Byzantium, and were to be an important factor in Islam. The Empire divided into two sees, Greek and Latin, recognizing that the Roman Church was effectively the government in that backwater while Constantinople was protected by the government. For a time, Alexandria was a seat of considerable sophistication in the realm of Byzantium.

In an amazing seventy years and beyond, much of the world and all of its institutions changed forever. A sword, Dhúl-Faqār, was put to the throat of Hindu, Christian and Jew to submit or die in the sweep of Islam from Spain to India. The promise that Ismael would be a great nation is fulfilled in Islam, the perfect institution in the service of Al-Lah.

Alexandria was gone: the loss of Byzantine lands wounded the Church born of saints and martyrs at Constantinople, while Rome fearing Islam without a shield of eastern protection made quick moves for new partners and protectors among the powerful Franks. It was first the pope and Pepin in 750 AD followed by a final joining of Church and State with the coronation of Charlemagne, Emperor of the Holy Roman Empire by Pope Leo III in Rome. It was done on Christmas day (Mithra-Saturnalia – sun god) and brought Christianized western Europe to the feet of Rome.

Constantinople and the Empire were under assault for centuries and so weakened as to invite a clever move for control by the Roman Church in excommunicating the Eastern Church in 1040 AD, which stands to the present. The last breath of that Church was taken 400 years later in 1453 when the city fell to Mehmed, while in Rome the pope offered prayers to no avail. Rome was now finally alone on top.

The date 1453 also marks a communication revolution with the advent of printing and thus ending the lock on the Bible held by the Church and freeing the individual to reading the truth in his own language. The revolution exploded in 1520 when Luther never backed down from Paul's position that salvation is by faith alone. In the following centuries to the present, a myriad of institutions of varying Christian thought developed and thrived.

Going back to the year 1200, the position of the Church seemed invincible. Pope Innocent III was effectively the emperor of Europe with all Catholic nations subject to him. Considerable wealth had occurred as crusaders slaughtered Jews in their long march to Palestine. Also, a flow of assets to the Church came from the estates of fallen crusaders. The pope authorized Venice to conduct another crusade to Palestine which went no further than Constantinople where the city was sacked and money made more safely than fighting muslims

This was a measure of the elite of the time but other strong forces were at work. In 1312, the Knights Templar had returned from Palestine with great wealth, a powerful organization, and pagan trappings such as prayer beads and a black madonna. Prayer beads could become the rosary for Miriam's intercession at death. The invading black madonna from the East was ingrained in the people's worship going back thousands of years with many names changes for both woman and the child. A black woman shown with a baby or a very young boy was the mother of the sun god, and this was grafted on the Christian story of Miriam and Jesus.

At this time, there were almost continuous fires roasting the flesh of thousands of heretics which were broadly defined as any person or organization that threatened government or Church. Cathars pursued a popular diversion from Catholic doctrine, and as a result were condemned by the Church to be slaughtered using as its agent, the forces of the French king. The Templars were branded heretics to have them qualified for extermination while their considerable wealth was divided between Church and king. Neither group exists today testifying that the constant lethal campaign against heresy was a success.

In Pope Innocent's time, there was an odd couple in two individuals that would be awarded sainthood. Dominic the Spaniard was relentless in the pursuit of heresy, cajoling or enforcing conversion to the *truth*. The other was Francis, the son of Peter the Roman, whose approach to truth was to live it. His humility and commitment to the

Christ was very popular with the lower class which was 90% of all. He probably died somewhat unhappy since Innocent seized on his popularity to institutionalize and control the presentation of his philosophy. The orders exist but does Francis?

By the nineteenth century the growth of secular ideologies had the popes under great pressure to maintain relevance and emotional connections. In 1871, Pius IX finally had the First Vatican Council officially declare that Miriam did not die but was raised directly into heaven in a glorified body. If the presumption of sinless perfection for her lifetime under Hebrew law was true, then she could not die. If she were perfectly sinless as was the Christ, she won the promise of God for life without death. This was now voted as absolute truth.

In the issue of power and relevance of the papacy, the resolution was managed with more contention. The pope required that the cardinals vote to establish his infallibility in faith and morals (his definition) but that raised a number of concerns on the part of the cardinals. Most saw this as the pope's move to consolidate power in himself and strip it away from the cardinals. A few may have considered that this revelation from God was problematic at best. Being at best, establishment politicians, the cardinals knew that a negative vote would be disaster for the institution, so they arranged to pass the legislation by one vote while 47 cardinals found it absolutely necessary to leave Rome before casting a vote: that's how it works!

Readers are now encouraged to think and choose between the two persons in this cosmic war that appears to be near the end of the engagement.

Epilogue

Some words from the writer:

Errors in the text are mine — the Author does not err.

I am an individual person and, by right, make choices for which I alone am responsible.

At the age of 40, I was drawn into a contract. In subsequent years and only in retrospect, it was made clear:

That I was never alone in my life;

That I was always protected;

The course set for me was never understood at the time.

I never prayed - was taught his prayers

I never asked for anything — got everything

I never had deep emotions — was taught to love and receive love

Hope the readers do as well or better.

Edward

www.ingramcontent.com/pod-product-compliance
Lightning Source LLC
Chambersburg PA
CBHW020941090426
42736CB00010B/1218